How to Overcome Procrastination

Overcoming Perfectionism and Anxiety to Break the Deadline Dilemma

Aria Ponder

Table of Contents

Introduction

Do you ever have that moment where you know you really should start your taxes...but this YouTube rabbit hole you fell into just seems more intriguing? What were you even supposed to be doing again?

We all procrastinate sometimes, but for chronic procrastinators, putting things off isn't just an occasional bad habit; it's a tendency that gets in the way of accomplishing our goals. We look at important responsibilities, and we don't feel motivated. And it would be fine, except then things start piling up around us as we're chilling with our pal denial, and suddenly we realize, "Oh right, I knew there was something I was supposed to be doing for the last month instead of spending time on less important tasks."

So why do we do this?

In this book, we're going to explore the reasons behind the chronic procrastinator's habits and thought patterns. We'll discover competing motivations wrestling for control, overprotective instincts trying to keep us safe, and pesky irrational tendencies screwing everything up. By studying the psychology up close, we can start to understand why, even when the rational, future-thinking side wants nothing more than to just get this project done already, that irrational side keeps getting in the way, dragging us onto YouTube instead.

Luckily, our exploration won't just be fascinating; it'll equip us with useful strategies against procrastination. We'll uncover productivity tricks, mindset shifts for overcoming perfectionism, and more mental tools designed to manage problematic tendencies. And we'll walk through real stories from former chronic procrastinators who managed to escape their clutches and make their dreams happen against the odds.

If you find yourself trapped between good intentions and poor follow-through, join me as we try to understand the procrastinating brain to gain more control over habits and make things happen. I think you'll find it's an enlightening journey well worth taking.

Chapter 1: Understanding Procrastination

Let's start at the very beginning: what is procrastination?

Procrastination is when you put off the things you need to do. Often, people peg it on laziness or even just bad time management. At its core, procrastination is an emotional regulation issue; it happens when feeling good right now feels more urgent than logical priorities.

Like if I really should do my homework today to turn it in on time. But scrolling social media for hours is more enjoyable than math formulas. So, I choose instant mood boosts over important tasks, even knowing it's unwise.

It's like a little voice saying: "Choose fun! Not work!" And it's hard to resist. Before I know it, it's 1 a.m. the night before my homework is due. Oops.

Now, we all procrastinate sometimes. But chronic procrastinators don't just delay the occasional chore; we avoid responsibility frequently.

Some myths:

Myth 1: It's poor time management, but procrastinators can look busy while avoiding what matters most.

Myth 2: It's laziness. Not so, we have big goals; we're just scared to pursue them.

Myth 3: Habits can't change. But science says with new tactics, we can retrain our brains over time.

We'll dispel more myths throughout the chapter. Let's explore why procrastinators act this way and how the habit controls thinking. Understanding is the first step to gaining more control over self-defeating patterns.

Journey Into the Procrastinator's Brain

Let's explore what drives procrastination in the brain. Think of different motivations, like little workers directing behaviors behind the scenes.

First, we have the rational mind. This represents the prefrontal cortex, which handles planning, organization, and focusing on future goals. We can envision the rational mind working in an office, surrounded by calendars mapping out objectives, vision boards capturing hopes and dreams, and endless Post-It note reminders of tasks and deadlines. It runs around motivated and focused, pushing us to take steps today to achieve tomorrow's ambitions.

Then there's our fun-seeking self. Its singular job is to keep us feeling good right now. It represents the part of the brain attuned to immediate pleasure and stimulation, constantly scanning our environment for quick hits of enjoyment. We can picture the fun-seeking self as a playful companion always trying to cheer us up in the moment, whether through funny videos, sweet snacks, chatting with friends, or other pick-me-ups. Its motto is "Feel happy now!"

You'll notice the fundamental tension between these two aspects of self—the rational mind laser-focused on long-term goals, and the fun-seeking self-craving instant gratification. This divergence primes the pump for procrastination anytime our fun-seeking self gains too much power over discipline and planning.

What causes this ascent of pleasurable distractions over rational priorities? Often, worries and self-doubts start whispering anxious thoughts and triggering discomfort. Things like, "Who do you think you are trying to start a business?" or "You're not smart enough to ace this exam." To avoid the sting of inadequacy or failure, keeping the fun-seeking self-pampered suddenly feels like the safest path. Escapism lets us sidestep the voices undermining our capabilities.

Does this make sense as an explanation for why procrastination happens? Even when our rational mind knows we should complete a task, those self-critical whispers can be so unnerving that distraction and denial take over instead. By understanding these competing motivations and inner voices, we gain important insights into procrastination's psychological underpinnings.

Now, let's continue our exploration by diving into more quirky corners of the chronic procrastinator's mindset!

Analyzing Our Procrastination Dance Moves

Now that we've explored the hidden psychological forces behind procrastination let's observe how this plays out in real-world behaviors. I call them our "procrastination dance moves," those silly avoidance tactics and distraction gimmicks that subtly sabotage progress.

Let's examine binge-watching Becky as a case study. Becky's ultimate life dream is to start a nonprofit organization that provides underprivileged kids with coding education and technology access. It's a beautiful vision fueled by her passions. However, whenever Becky actually sits down to work on the concrete first steps, like crafting a business plan or researching startup costs, this weird anxiety starts bubbling up inside.

Before she knows it, Becky finds herself 10 episodes deep into some random Netflix series, eyes glazed over, mouth covered in chip dust and Queso stains. She snaps out of her binge-watching trance for a brief moment, suddenly jolting up and shouting aloud, "My life's purpose!" But then...she repeats this agonizing and avoidant cycle. Every. Single. Time.

Or what about our friend hyperfocused Hannah? Hannah becomes wholly obsessed and wrapped up in seemingly "easier" or less personally intimidating tasks any time her anxiety-provoking, big-picture passion project comes up. Last Tuesday, for example, rather than outline the children's book she dreams of writing, Hannah fell into a rabbit hole of reorganizing old photos and mementos that lasted over 20 hours. The weekend before that, she awoke with inspiration at 3 a.m. and proceeded to deep-clean her oven rather than brainstorm her book ideas. Yeah, not exactly rocking the productivity scales there.

The point is, when we closely observe these mental distraction dances and avoidance behaviors in action, we start to notice some clear patterns. The patterns allow us to temporarily numb difficult emotions, self-soothe anxiety, and postpone daunting but meaningful priority tasks. Psychologists actually have a name for this collection of delay tendencies—they call them "global behavioral delay patterns."

These patterns often become almost unconscious habits over time, resulting in procrastination that consistently derails goals and dreams without us even realizing why we're stuck or where to start. Pretty sly and insidious, right? But only once we actively recognize and bring these patterns into consciousness can we start to disrupt the dances intentionally and create new moves.

Recognizing Behaviors

Now we understand the psychology behind procrastination and the avoidance behaviors it leads to. But what actually triggers these counterproductive patterns?

As we explore further, we find the procrastinator's psyche littered with undermining voices and critical inner monologues. Fear voice. Boredom voice. Insecurity voice. They lurk inside, ready to whisper discouraging or alarming things.

As soon as they murmur anxiously, "Who do you think you are to try that?" or "This task is pointless," we hastily leap into distraction dances for relief.

Anything to quiet the voices undercutting our capabilities! YouTube to numb the sting! Snacks to self-soothe! We scarcely notice when distraction-seeking hardens into reflexive cycles, keeping us from meaningful goals.

Other times, no overt criticisms arise. Our minds have become so accustomed to questioning ourselves preemptively that we instinctively avoid important tasks before seriously attempting them. Either way, identifying these undermining inner voices provides huge insight into why procrastination persists.

So, let's get familiar with those voices. Maybe an unreasonable expectation whisperer insists you should handle everything perfectly? Or does an imposter voice say you lack qualifications?

Pinpointing our voices robs them of mystique and power. Then, they morph into mundane obstacles to be dealt with rather than terrifying specters. Ready? Shedding light on inner critics is the first step toward quieting and overcoming them.

The Procrastination Cycle

We've explored why procrastinators avoid things and what triggers counterproductive coping behaviors. But procrastination reinforces itself in a troublesome cycle.

Imagine a student filled with inspiration, declaring, "I will start tutoring disadvantaged youth!" But soon, doubt encroaches... "Who am I to do that?" Their confidence wavers.

Fear of failure emerges. They cope by binge-watching shows. Time disappears.

As deadlines rush closer with no progress made, panic sets in. More avoidance and distraction follow to numb stress—more potential wasted.

Soon, our once-inspired student is surrounded by remnants of distraction, barely connecting to their vision. The farther they descend into the cycle, the less capable they feel until even basic steps seem beyond reach.

This cycle explains how generations of aspirations have withered. Stuck in anxiety and avoidance, people lose momentum, needing only a nudge to regain traction.

The path forward is clear: we must unravel ourselves from this unproductive loop! By recognizing its stages, we can catch ourselves sooner and redirect energy toward goals. Tiny steps add up if consistently pursued. With vigilance, we can ascend from stagnancy to meaningful progress.

Getting Our Sherlock On— Clues to Crack Our Cases

We've done good investigative work unraveling the procrastinator's mindset. Now, let's channel that insight to reflect on our own habits.

Grab your journal, we're going pattern hunting!

Do you notice any avoidance dance moves resembling Becky's distraction rollercoaster? Or clusters of those delaying behaviors therapists often mention? Patterns like obsessive organizing or escapist fantasizing whenever something intimidates us?

Let's examine this to-do list: "Finish coding course, set wedding date, book doctor physical." But every task is crossed out, replaced by "Marathon TV show...again."

It seems our hero was on the cusp of progress before old habits rerouted them. What happened to cause his plans to go off track?

Often, anxiety spikes right when we try to be productive, triggering paralyzing doubts. Those familiar whispers may have emerged: "You'll never actually succeed at this goal" or "You're too disorganized for big projects." Discouragement leads us back to what feels safer: binge-watching instead of trying.

By spotting these personal patterns, what sets off our stress, and where it leads us—we gain the power to intercept the cycle sooner next time rather than be controlled by it.

Let's turn insight into action: What are your unique procrastination flavors and triggers? Once we know the "what and why," we can learn strategies to short-circuit what holds us back at the source. Our inner Sherlocks are on the case!

The Impact on Mental Health

We've investigated why people chronically avoid important tasks. Powerful insights.

But an important question emerges: How might all this avoidance impact us mentally in the long-term? Clearly, it obstructs goals and sparks frustration. But what are the deeper psychological effects?

The bad news is procrastination can truly undermine mental health, increasing anxiety, torpedoing self-worth, and more. The good news? Once we recognize unhealthy patterns, we can start dismantling them with some brain retraining!

First, the science. When we compulsively distract from meaningful goals repeatedly, the brain thinks, "I must avoid this because it's truly threatening."

Over time, even small progress steps seem scary and impossible! Motivation drains as we normalize, hiding in quick dopamine spurts rather than pushing forward.

Research confirms chronic procrastinators have higher cortisol and lower self-esteem (Yan & Zhang, 2022). We tend to be more depressed and self-critical. This makes sense because continually betraying our own interests doesn't feel great.

While occasional distraction is no big deal, this habit can sabotage mental well-being over time. The more we understand this, the sooner we can catch and redirect counterproductive tendencies.

Before progressing further, let me dispel some common misconceptions about procrastinators:

Myth 1: Procrastinators are irresponsible and lazy.

False! Procrastinators actually have ambitions that are equally as high as those of non-procrastinators. However, they often feel overwhelmed when facing large, intimidating tasks. Rather than laziness, procrastination often stems from the feeling that a task is too big or complex to tackle. So procrastinators delay starting tasks out of feeling overwhelmed, not due to being work-averse or irresponsible. This is a significant and important difference in understanding the root causes behind procrastination.

Myth 2: Procrastination is an innate personality flaw.

False! Studies prove this thinking pattern is a learned habit we can retrain, not some inherent defect. We simply need proper support and techniques for reshaping behavior.

Myth 3: It's just an issue of poor time management.

Super false! We tend to be masters at "looking busy" while dodging real priorities through distraction and avoidance dances. What we need most is guidance on regulating emotions, not more scheduling tips!

It feels good to clarify things. For too long, people blamed character without acknowledging the nuanced emotional knots perpetuating delay habits.

But now we understand the intricate psychology behind procrastination. So, we're perfectly positioned to transform things with self-compassion and the right strategies. Growth awaits!

By busting myths, we clear space for progress. Let's continue exposing limiting lies while cultivating our untapped potential! The path is there if we take it step by step.

Overcoming Perfectionism

Many procrastinators also struggle with perfectionism. This means setting extremely high standards for performance that feel impossible to reach. So we put things off over and over, waiting for the "perfect moment" to start that never comes.

Perfectionism sets us up to fail because no first draft or initial attempt will ever be flawless right away. And research shows that fear of not being excellent paralyzes taking action at all. It leads to chronic avoidance (Swider et al., 2018).

We have to give ourselves permission to let ideas unfold through repeated attempts over time. Think of athletes, musicians, and writers; they don't wake up flawless at their craft. Mastery gets built slowly through practice and learning from mistakes.

Shifting to value consistent effort, not perfect outcomes right away, makes creating possible again.

Try writing two messy diary paragraphs daily without judging them. Feel the freedom to return, just accumulating pages over weeks. Track progress quantitatively, not qualitatively. Volume leads to voice.

Likewise, painters commit simply to filling canvases with color during timed creation intervals rather than fixating on museum-worthy compositions straightaway. Unleash your creativity, figuring things out as you go.

Across endeavors, frame progress as improving through patience rather than demanding instant trophies. Savor small gains proving capability expanding through courageous craftsmanship. Let go of perfectionist pressures that make even small steps feel frightening. The path ahead opens by valuing each imperfect step nonetheless.

Keep marching forward boldly through the fog. Direction matters more than speed when overcoming fear. Consistency builds the confidence necessary to break through creative barriers so intrinsic genius can shine bright.

You already hold everything necessary for mastery within. Progress requires simply planting one foot ahead of the other until momentum carries dreams forward victorious.

Cultivating Self-Compassion

Battling procrastination also requires meeting setbacks with self-compassion, not harsh criticism making things worse. By speaking to ourselves with understanding around growth areas, we stay motivated to keep trying. Progress flows from patience.

What is self-compassion? It means relating to ourselves kindly like we would a good friend struggling with something. We don't insult them as a failure or reject them as flawed. We offer empathy, encouragement, and support.

Research shows talking to ourselves this way transforms habit change and achievement journeys that once seemed impossible (Vedantam, 2023). Self-criticism fuels avoidance cycles, further delaying progress when we need it most. It tricks the brain into perceiving threats and futility everywhere. Suddenly, even minimal steps feel terrifying.

But self-directed warmth short-circuits this self-defeating process. We frame missteps as signaling areas for skill building through compassionate effort. Challenges become shared chapters in the human journey rather than confirming personal deficiencies. Struggle feels navigable.

Practically, how do we cultivate this crucial self-compassion muscle when inner critics run raging?

Start small, gently catching, then reframing harsh judgments into understanding and encouragement. Write supportive phrases you would offer a struggling friend, then read them aloud to yourself as if discovering inherent worth for the first time.

Do regular meditations envisioning negative self-talk as passing clouds rather than truth. Allow difficult emotions space without believing the stories attached. Bring caring attention back to the present moment again and again.

Consistency builds trust in capability more than instant miracles judged against unrealistic standards. Procrastination loses power when we patiently parent ourselves through incremental forward movement. You've got this!

Case Studies

Meet Henry, accountant extraordinaire at the Acme Company...when he manages to show up. Henry dreamed of getting his CPA certification for years but always put off studying until the annual exam rolled around and panic set in. He'd then pull all-nighters for weeks, cramming material he could've gradually learned.

Henry avoided taking the test after suffering multiple panic attacks over failing. It wasn't until his colleague Marina made an offhand comment about signing up for a CPA prep course together that something clicked. Having an accountability buddy ignited Henry's motivation not to let her down.

Pairing up to study a few nights weekly, their camaraderie eased test anxiety and improved retention, too! Henry finally passed the beastly exam handily on his first attempt. Moral: External motivators can turn the tide of procrastination!

Or examine, Zoe, a talented sculptor whose room overflowed with half-finished clay models, but none complete enough for gallery openings. Perfectionism always stopped her short of finishing any piece. "What if it's not good enough?" she'd fret endlessly.

The tipping point came after Zoe shelved her largest work-in-progress yet, a breathtaking human torso cradling a moon. Right as she muffled creativity's call yet again, a pang of regret hit deep.

Zoe asked herself, "If I don't start putting my soul's creations out into the world just as they are, will I ever truly live?" The answer was obvious. She promised herself then on to transit each sculpture from conception to completion, no matter how imperfect, and finally began sharing her gifts proudly.

Exercise: Self Reflect

What stood out to you most as you read about the psychology and cycles of procrastination? Was anything surprising or illuminating?

Looking inward, can you identify any "procrastination dance moves" or avoidance tendencies in your own behaviors? What activities do you repeatedly turn to when feeling anxious or overwhelmed?

See if you can pinpoint a few of your triggering voices that tend to undermine your motivation and derail progress. What specific worries or criticisms do they whisper? How might you start quieting those voices?

How might procrastination and distraction seeking be impacting your mental health and well-being over the long run? What shifts might create better alignment between your short-term actions and long-term dreams?

Journal Exercise:
Make a two-column table. On the left, write down three to five goals or dreams you keep delaying. On the right, dig into

why you procrastinate on each one. Identify underlying fears, perceived obstacles, and frustrations with the process. See what insights emerge!

Affirmation:

"I have everything within me to achieve my dreams through incremental progress."

Action Step:

Commit to a small action aligned with one avoided goal. Maybe outline one chapter idea, enroll in a class, or set up a meeting about the project. Don't shoot for perfection; just get momentum!

Wrapping Up...

We've uncovered a lot about the psychology behind procrastination, from its subtle emotional roots to the unproductive patterns it pulls us into.

But now comes the constructive part, it's time to apply this knowledge and steer toward focused productivity so we can achieve our meaningful goals!

I don't know about you, but I'm tired of letting twisted myths, anxious doubts, and distracting tendencies obstruct my dreams. Now that we recognize how procrastination subtly influences thinking, we can dismantle those barriers step-by-step.

Imagine finally breaking free of useless time-wasting and taking consistent action on what matters most. That reality is possible, friends!

Here are key insights:

- Procrastination stems from emotional regulation challenges, not character flaws. It happens when short-term mood repair feels more compelling than long-term thinking.

- Vicious cycles where anxiety feeds avoidance can quickly spiral out of control if we don't catch them.

- But we can retrain habits through motivational tools and self-awareness!

And some helpful starting strategies:

- pinpoint your procrastination triggers

- schedule distraction time

- rally an accountability crew

- reframe fear of failure as an opportunity for growth

Plus, much more. For now, let's take that first step toward focused productivity and fulfillment. Progress awaits!

Chapter 2: Consequences of Procrastination

In the previous chapter, we explored the tangled psychological roots of procrastination—from emotional regulation challenges to vicious anxiety cycles that can trap us. Now, we'll shine a spotlight on the ripple effects that chronic delay habits can have in multiple areas of life.

It's crucial we investigate the consequences to fully grasp procrastination's gravity. Often, we blow off tasks, assuming putting them off a bit won't matter much. However, researchers have consistently shown that perseverant procrastination correlates to some heavy outcomes down the line, academically, professionally, financially, and psychologically (Visser et al., 2018).

Of course, procrastination doesn't impact every person the exact same way. We all have different goals, environments, obligations, and breaking points. But whether you currently struggle with minor tardiness or all-consuming avoidance cycles, understanding the proven costs of chronic procrastination can provide motivation to nip delay habits sooner rather than later.

So, in this chapter, we'll walk through some top domains where pernicious procrastination causes the most dysfunction, from torpedoed productivity to strained relationships, fiscal irresponsibility, derailed opportunities, and more. My hope is not to scare you with doom-and-gloom scenarios! But rather bring sober awareness to why addressing chronic delay now can prevent exponential harm down the road. Let's dive in.

Immediate Impact on Performance

Let's start with the clearest, most instant consequence: how procrastination directly hinders task completion. When we chronically put things off until the last minute, output and performance inevitably suffer for multiple reasons.

First, delaying getting started leaves less total time to work on a project before deadlines hit. Cramming everything into the final hours prevents us from fully developing ideas or creating the highest quality work we're capable of. Nuance, polish, and thoughtful organization go out the window.

Second, waiting until the last minute also means we lose opportunities that come with time flexibility. When assignments or preparations stack up unfinished for weeks, we miss chances to get feedback, adjust the course based on new learnings, or simply space out intensive effort. By holding off, we limit our iteration capabilities.

Finally, frenzied rush jobs sparked by procrastination often correlate to more mistakes and oversights. When we finally start under pressing time constraints, stress clouds our brain power, leading to silly errors that proper planning may have prevented.

Beyond degrading the quality of individual assignments, these dynamics compound over time to sabotage academic and professional success. Consistently turning things in late threatens grades and performance reviews. Botching tasks erode trust and credibility. Lost opportunities and flawed outputs prevent us from showcasing our true talents.

The key takeaway? Procrastination immediately undercuts personal achievement by depriving efforts of time, iteration, and mental clarity. While an occasional delay may be no big deal, chronic tardiness can slowly degrade results, reputation, and advancement in demonstrable ways. Let's steer clear of this preventable pitfall!

Strain on Mental Health

Beyond tangible performance metrics, persistent procrastination also takes a toll psychologically in the form of cascading stress, anxiety, and diminished self-worth. This emotional impact gets overlooked but can be just as damaging long-term.

It starts with the perpetual tension between obligations we know we should complete and the prospect of feeling discomfort in the process. As commitments like work projects or paperwork pile up unfinished, a fog of background anxiety takes root, keeping us in a constant state of unease.

This anxiety compounds each time we employ short-term relief mechanisms like distraction or denial rather than tackling responsibilities head-on. Mental anguish grows as the gap between our actions and intentions widens. We end up feeling perpetually dissatisfied with both our output and our inability to control counterproductive habits.

Over time, repeatedly betraying our own goals and values erodes self-trust and confidence. Thoughts like "What's wrong with me that I can't just sit down and do this basic task?" seep into self-talk, serving only to exacerbate delays. Soon, reluctance morphs into shame and despair.

Research corroborates this unhealthy cycle; those who chronically procrastinate report higher stress, more depression, and amplified pessimism, along with severely lowered self-esteem compared to non-procrastinators (Beutel et al., 2016).

Clearly, putting things off repeatedly not only impedes results, but it also secretly drags mental health through the mud in insidious ways. Let's safeguard internal well-being by keeping tasks and priorities from piling out of control! Our future selves will thank us.

Implications for Relationships

Beyond inner turmoil, chronically avoiding important tasks and duties can also take an interpersonal toll, putting strain on relationships. Procrastination breeds resentment on both sides over time.

In professional domains, consistency and accountability matter. Colleagues rely on each other to pull their weight on shared goals. When we repeatedly drop the ball on projects or miss deadlines, the burden falls on others to pick up the slack. Not only does this foster frustration and lose trust, it also weakens critical work relationships.

In personal contexts like family or friendships, procrastination signals a similar disregard for other's time and efforts. If we perpetually show up late, delay commitments, or stall on promises for loved ones, sentiment erodes. They reasonably doubt our ability to follow through when needed.

This habitual flaking has deeper emotional implications, too. Often, when tasks pile up undone, it's because we prioritized short-term mood boosts over important long-term aims shared with partners or relatives. The disconnect between actions and espoused values breeds resentment on both sides over time.

In summary, chronically breaking commitments gradually undermines rapport & mutual regard in any relationship. If connections matter, then diligently taking care of responsibilities signals the respect others deserve—at home, at work, and beyond. The peace of mind is priceless.

So, not only does tackling procrastination serve us personally, but it strengthens bonds across contexts. By facing discomfort and handling business promptly, we invest in relationships that make all the difference.

Missed Opportunities and Career Implications

Thus far, we've covered immediate performance hits, psychological strain, and frayed relationships spawned by procrastination. But the business realm, in particular, reveals another long-term consequence: missed opportunities for advancement. Delays can sabotage careers over decades.

Every small responsibility dodged, or deadline missed plants seeds of distrust in supervisors' minds. "If they can't handle X task now, can I truly depend on them to spearhead major initiatives down the road?" Leaders hesitate before offering stretch assignments to chronic procrastinators.

Simultaneously, putting things off causes us to miss chances to showcase our talents. Job opportunities that got away, brilliant proposals set aside, skill-building courses never completed, lost openings to get noticed.

Over years in the workforce, these dynamics compound. Consistent high performers rise to the top—the unreliable plateau to mediocrity. Before we know it, entire career trajectories pivot on habits forged early on.

Of course, sometimes procrastination springs from environments misaligned with natural talents or passions. In those cases, chronically uncompleted goals may signal the need for a major change rather than piecemeal improvements.

But regardless of context, unlocking our potential requires facing down whatever stops us from bringing our best efforts consistently, whether inner barriers or external forces. Sustained diligence pays exponentially. The time is now to start.

Diminished Life Satisfaction

As we've explored, giving in to delay habits exacts a high cost across domains, from productivity to relationships and beyond. But an overarching consequence eclipses discrete failures: Procrastination can drain life's very meaning when dreams chronically go unpursued.

It's one thing to flake on an assignment and resolve to recover. It's another to repeatedly sabotage personal goals year after year until our presumed potential feels like a myth. Unfinished creative projects, abandoned athletic aspirations, relationships unattended to, and missed milestones compound.

Like a guitarist with broken strings unable to strum beloved songs or a runner with stones in her shoes abandoning races, we stand dismayed by the growing gap between who we envision ourselves to be and how we actually spend our fleeting days.

Indeed, longitudinal research reveals procrastinators report significantly lower overall well-being and life satisfaction compared to disciplined peers when surveyed in later years (Beutel et al., 2016). Unactualized visions gnaw at us. Regret haunts.

Of course, satisfaction stems from fulfillment beyond achievement in family, faith, or service. But most of us hold dear a few life dreams requiring sustained effort over time. When habitual delay subverts those journeys, our souls notice. Vitality drains.

Now for the good news: change remains possible at any age. By cultivating self-awareness around why we stall, combined with consistent baby steps forward, we can resuscitate dreams long forgotten. Our future still awaits.

Financial Consequences

So far, we've covered heavy quality-of-life costs fueled by delay, fraying productivity, confidence, relationships, and meaning itself. One final domain worth mentioning, given most goals require resources, is how procrastination sabotages financial health.

First, putting things off often directly prevents asset accrual. Cash flow stalls when we hesitate on lucrative side projects or drag our feet on career-accelerating classes (common delay domains for aspiring entrepreneurs or creatives). Income plateaued is earnings lost.

Similarly, indecision leads to missed investment windfalls all the time. Whether hesitating on a hot stock tip or waiting too long to buy into a high-growth real estate market, timing matters. Equity gains missed don't get redone.

Beyond opportunity costs, active financial penalties also arise. Paying late fees for dragging on bills and paperwork is common. Far worse is blowing deadlines for scholarships, insurance applications, or tax deductions. That's literally cash walking out the door unnecessarily because we didn't handle business.

And interest costs rack up fast once delay intersects, needing loans for big purchases or emergencies. Poor credit from mismanaged finances begets more pricey debt obligations. It compounds quickly.

In summation, dollars correlate directly to discipline. Income earned and savings maximized rely partly on hustling, not overworking, but following through on identified opportunities in a timely way. Just as procrastination sabotages the achievement of life dreams, it undermines building the financial runway to get there.

Let's start recognizing costly delays and redirecting actions sooner rather than later. Our wallet and dreams will thank us for it!

Overcoming Perfectionism Ripple Effects

Many procrastinators struggle with perfectionism, too. This means setting super high standards for performance that feel impossible to reach. So we put things off over and over, waiting for the perfect moment that never comes.

Perfectionism's Impact Over Time

At first, perfectionism convinces us we're protecting work quality by endlessly tweaking and analyzing before sharing. But in reality, it cripples results by preventing output entirely. Months lost chasing flawlessness means declining productivity plus mounting anxiety as deliverables stall. Confidence plummets alongside credibility when little gets finished, permeating most areas soon enough.

Additionally, harboring rigidly high personal standards often correlates with believing we deeply disappoint close ones through normal human struggle. So, beyond eroding professional stats, perfectionism strains relationships through avoidance and secrecy instead of interdependence. We isolate rather than risk judgment by revealing struggles. Resentment brews on both sides as years pass, ardently maintaining a facade of having everything under control. Friendships and romance suffer without vulnerability.

Ironically, income and advancement often stagnate, too, despite the external impression of elite competence. Sidelining creative risks for "guaranteed" moneymakers means lost innovation opportunities that may have won fortune and fame. We lose inroads to upper echelons requiring bold vision over flawless reputation. Company ladders pass us by opting for predictable stability and pigeonholing potential. Safe now loses big later.

In summary, perfectionism's short-term illusion of quality output gives way to long-term mediocrity across domains from stalled productivity to superficial relationships and middle-class living. Our present overfunctioning sets up future underachieving.

Shifting From Perfect to Progress

Thankfully, a simple mindset shift from perfect to progress kicks this delay reaction into growth gear. The antidote? Valuing small gains made consistently over time versus instant monumental feats. Mini habits build a journey to joy!

For example, by journaling two paragraphs daily without judging prose, pages soon fill. Tracking progress feels fulfilling versus evaluating talent. Writing becomes identity, not rating. The language flows imperfectly but unceasingly.

Likewise, musicians transform rehearsal struggles into stage readiness by understanding mastery as iterative, not instant. Each practice session builds skill bricks erecting careers.

We relate to setbacks similarly after shifting from perfectionism to flexible growth. Not personal failings but informational signals revealing where higher reaches require sturdier support structures. Iterative tweaks summon our best.

Across domains, progress is defined by patience with gradual gains that accumulate exponential fruits in time. Savor slightly better rather than demand perfect. Allow work and relationships to grow through consistency, not miracles judged against unrealistic standards. Your life gets revolutionized by progress, one small courageous step forward at a time!

Cultivating Compassion to Combat Shame

Beyond cementing constructive mindsets, conquering procrastination also requires meeting inevitable backslides with self-compassion, not merciless criticism exacerbating shame cycles and further delaying progress.

Shame Triggers Avoidance

When we internally degrade perceived laziness, distraction tendencies, or failure to complete goals by prescribed timelines, toxic shame often swells, casting us as hopeless procrastinators doomed forever. Harsh self-judgment feels temporarily motivating, intending to spark grit through guilt. But truly, it fuels avoidance and paralysis, amplifying problems exponentially.

You see, shame fundamentally convinces us that the entirety of who we are remains defective, not conditional behaviors needing improvement. So why attempt better habits if they are inherently broken? Psychologists find shame's global indictments correlate with procrastination most since no achievement disproves personal inadequacy nagging internally. We flee spotlights, inevitably confirming suspected fraudulence.

Compassion Cultivates Change

Alternatively, speaking to ourselves with affectionate understanding around growth edges alleviates shame's suffocating grip. We view periodic delays or distraction tendencies as signaling areas for skill building through compassionate effort. It's not about indictment but iteration.

For example, "I struggled to complete that project on time. My energy levels may need support. Let me try working in smaller chunks with self-care breaks. Each piece finished brings me closer to excellence."

Here, self-talk emotionally regulates frustration into constructive strategy pivots, teaching our brains crawling precedes walking. There are no bad people, only undeveloped skills. Progress flows from patience. Additionally, framing struggles as relatable rather than isolating neutralizes shame. Challenges become shared chapters in the human journey rather than confirming peculiar personal limitations. We suffer well together.

In total, combatting reflexive self-condemnation with rising rates of self-compassion kills procrastination's parasitic food source. Judge, not the timing, but nurture the trying. Your mess indeed becomes your message, modeling growth possibilities for fellow travelers once we voice journeys with courage.

Case Studies: Unveiling the Ripple Effect

We've now extensively analyzed research on common domains impacted when procrastination goes unchecked: productivity, wellness, relationships, missed chances, and money. But how do these consequences converge in real people's lives? Let's bring the costs to life through a few case studies.

Meet Sam, a talented marketing consultant who consistently scored top performance reviews for winning multi-million dollar clients for his firm. But Sam harbored entrepreneurial dreams outside his nine-to-five, often brainstorming late into the night about how to launch his own digital agency.

The only problem? For years, Sam failed to follow through on his brilliant business ideas long enough to build tangible momentum. His journal overflowed with half-finished websites abandoned marketing funnels, and course content he dreamt up but never completed. Sam couldn't seem to push past resistance points.

Over months and years, his stalled progress spawned a cascade of consequences: mounting anxiety and self-doubt, unraveling confidence despite surface-level career success, strained connection with his wife who longed to support his calling and missed income from pursuits that could free Sam to work for himself. Procrastination's ripple effect ravaged all fronts.

Or examine Allison, a fitness instructor who saw stellar client transformations when she put effort into updated workout plans. But for ages, Allison dragged on developing an online training portal other coaches used successfully for passive income. After years of rationalizing, "I'm just too busy with back-to-back classes," Allison saw the market peak and competitors lock in ecosystem dominance. Her income plateaued indefinitely.

In both cases, early initiative deficits spawned exponential lost opportunities over time, along with psychological, relational, and financial consequences, too.

The good news? By getting support to overcome internal and external obstacles now, both Sam and Allison can begin actualizing long-held visions before it becomes "too late," because when it comes to realizing dreams, it's never too late to start.

Exercise: Self Reflect

Which potential consequence or cost of chronic procrastination resonates most with you currently: fraying productivity, anxiety, strained relationships, career stagnancy, financial issues, or general life dissatisfaction?

Make a list of two to three goals or dreams you've consistently put off pursuing over the years. Then, brainstorm how delaying each one may have impacted other domains like mental health, connections, missed opportunities, etc., in cascading ways. What insights emerge?

Think of someone you know struggling with chronic procrastination and avoidance. From what you can tell, what are some tangible consequences they may be facing due to delaying priorities?

Journaling Exercise:

Make a T-chart. On the left side, write two to three goals you keep putting off. On the right, journal about how you envision accomplishing those aspirations might positively transform things like your confidence, productivity, finances, connections, and overall life satisfaction.

Notice if visualizing future benefits creates more urgency to take action today, even if starting small.

Affirmation:

"My consistent progress generates compounding returns over time."

Action Step:

Commit to one micro-step aligned with a stalled goal. It could be a Google search, signing up for a course, or having a conversation to get accountability. Just get momentum!

Wrapping Up...

We've now extensively analyzed the ripple effect from chronic procrastination across life domains, including:

- botched performance and missed achievements

- spiraling anxiety, stress, and diminished self-regard

- fraying relationships as commitments go unmet

- lost advancement opportunities over the years

- mounting financial penalties

- putting off pursuing our dreams collectively robs life of meaning

Putting things off consistently doesn't just briefly delay outcomes, it compounds consequences exponentially over time.

But before despair sets in, the good news is small shifts can massively change trajectories, even for lifelong procrastinators. We can circumvent exponential costs by cultivating self-awareness around our specific avoidance triggers and then strategically building momentum with external support.

Sometimes, the most brilliant ideas stay locked inside, never emerging to meet their potential and change lives. The world misses out all because fear of failure muzzled someone afraid to start.

But by understanding your triggers, getting accountability, and taking baby steps forward, our dreams suddenly glimmer and become tangible once more. The consequences of procrastination meet their mighty rival: human resilience.

Chapter 3:
The Science of
Motivation

What drives someone to labor for years in obscurity before their vision catches fire in the world? Or compels ordinary people to persist through rejection and obstacles that would deter most? The fuel behind such tenacity is good old motivation, humanity's engine revving passion and grit when called upon.

In this chapter, we'll crack open the science illuminating motivation's inner workings, both what steers us toward goals relentlessly as well as where momentum breaks down (hello, procrastination). Mastering this landscape allows us to optimize our own internal combustion to vaporize excuses and catalyze dreams with gusto!

We'll explore the psychology, neurology, and emotion regulation tricks that kick determination into high gear. Then, we'll analyze common pitfalls like perfectionism that gunk up the gears. Translating theory into action, we'll also provide tools for structuring little wins that stack up milestones en route to visions that once loomed impossibly distant.

Introduction to Motivation Science

We've explored how procrastination works and the costs of chronic delay. Now, let's discuss how to drive action instead of avoidance.

The key is understanding motivation's psychological underpinnings. With some science-backed tweaks, we can redirect energy toward goals, so progress sparks zeal rather than fear. We become those motivated people tackling big quests with gusto, astonishing couch potato friends. Yes, you can transform too.

But first, a crash course on motivation mechanics that run beneath our awareness and shape our actions. We'll peek inside the brain, lighting up when dreams feel irresistible, decode how intrinsic and extrinsic motivators collaborate to drive us, and explore research on resisting inertia versus summoning energy for breakthroughs.

Demystifying motivation's operating system allows us to troubleshoot precisely what hijacks our own aspirations. We shift willpower from a limited strength model to a renewable power source, electrifying dreams. If we learn how to flip the switch judiciously,

So whether you're battling chronic delay or simply want unbeatable determination, let's illuminate science-based motivational tactics. Progress awaits those wielding knowledge of the psyche's mysteries.

Psychological Factors in Motivation

What makes us burn the midnight oil on a project or compulsively persist against the odds? Let's unpack key psychological motivators.

Intrinsic Motivation

This drive comes from within when something feels naturally interesting or purposeful. Like reading about our favorite topic or mastering a beloved skill. Curiosity and growth often intrinsically compel us to persist at tasks. Even without external rewards, the process itself drives engagement when we have intrinsic motivation.

Extrinsic Motivation

External rewards also power motivation through reinforcement. Things like money, acclaim, or avoiding punishment can incentivize us, too. Grades for completing assignments, prizes for winning competitions, accountability check-ins to avoid letting others down, all of these leverage extrinsic motivation. We want the end result rather than enjoying the process itself, yet these constructs keep us dedicated.

Goal-Setting

Aligning activities with a meaningful outcome anchors effort as well. Goals help manifest visions, quantifying milestones that let us mark progress. Simply tracking incremental progress itself becomes rewarding and reinforcing. Having definable goals propels motivation.

Rewards

Relatedly, recognizing effort and progress delivers dopamine hits to our receptors—small treats like watching an episode after milestones celebrate baby steps and can positively reinforce habits. In fact, the psychology of random or unpredictable reinforcement has been shown to intensely amplify motivation through heightened anticipation.

Beliefs

Our guiding philosophies and assumptions also incentivize what actions we take. For example, do we see intelligence as fixed/rigid or elastic/growable through grit? Is the status quo intractable or malleable? Our core beliefs alter what possibilities we perceive and shape what we ultimately strive for.

Attitudes

More narrowly, feeling positively or negatively about a specific task fuels persistence. Perceiving something as useless, painfully boring, or overwhelmingly difficult quickly sabotages drive. But alternatively, sensing achievable challenges, purpose, and progress in something plants seeds of inspiration that blossom into perseverance. Our attitude toward the task predicts motivation.

Now armed with these psychology fundamentals, we can optimize motivation factors to propel ourselves past procrastination land into a productivity paradise.

Neurological Mechanisms That Drive Motivation

Psychological drivers clearly influence motivation, but behind the scenes, our brain circuitry amplifies these effects exponentially. Let's illuminate key neurological actors steering behavior.

The Brain's Reward System

At motivation's core lies the mesolimbic pathway, our brain's reward infrastructure funneling dopamine to incite action. When anticipating or experiencing something enjoyable, this circuitry fires, compelling us to stay engaged and continue to repeat that experience again and again. We feel intrinsically drawn toward activities lighting these up.

Neurotransmitters Influencing Motivation

Specifically, chemicals like dopamine, serotonin, and oxytocin surge when we perceive rewards. Dopamine floods in when a goal seems within reach, energizing zealous pursuit. Serotonin levels regulate how quickly rewards satisfy us before we need another hit. Finding the right rhythms actively sculpts motivation.

Habits and Neural Pathways

The more we repeat behaviors, the more ingrained their pathways become in our brains. Echoing activity strengthens synapses, laying the foundation for habits. Soon, just imagining delicious pasta fires signals toward related reward centers. This automaticity steers motivation one nibble at a time!

In summary, by linking tasks to innate reward circuits, we can neurologically embed inspiration where once only resistance reigned. This biological builder's blueprint allows for reconstructing motivation from the basement up.

How Emotions Shape Motivation

Beyond machinery whirring inside our skulls, let's examine how subjective experiences like emotions influence drive. After all, we're not robots, and as the procrastination abyss illustrated in technicolor detail, feelings often override systems. So, how can emotions propel rather than obstruct progress when harnessed properly?

How Negative Emotions Drain Motivation

It's obvious how negative mind states undermine action, depression breeds lethargy while anxiety triggers wheel-spinning analyzer paralysis. Even milder displeasures like boredom quickly sap momentum once we perceive tasks as meaningless or tedious chores. When unpleasant emotions take root, inspiration gets strangled.

Strategies for Managing Negative Emotional Barriers

Luckily, behavioral research reveals techniques for circumventing dreariness. Reappraising tasks as valuable development, infusing variety mid-project to restore curiosity, linking work to a higher purpose, tracking progress visually, and rewarding milestones all reconnect us to intrinsic satisfactions that anxiety obscures.

Leveraging Positive Emotions to Fuel Motivation

Beyond battling negatives, we can amplify helpful mind states, too. Experiencing autonomy, competency, and connectedness to others have proven motivating effects. Setting vivid goals conjures determination organically through imagination's power. Recognizing even micro-wins builds tiny crescendos of confidence, lifting spirits. Basically, by toggling emotional channels from draining to energizing flavors, we guide motivation's flow.

So, in summary, emotion and drive intertwine intimately, but with finesse, we can learn to conduct inner symphonies toward inspiration rather than indifference.

Understanding Procrastination as Motivation Gone Awry

Now armed with psychological and biological mechanisms steering motivation, let's bring this lens back to the procrastination conundrum's paralyzing potential. Why do we so often lose steam halfway to dreams? Motivational breakdowns.

How Motivation Deficits Drive Delay

When emotions bottleneck an endeavor's flow or rewards continue to seem nonexistent, once-clear goals fog over. Initiative falters without reinforcement, especially internally. Self-doubt seeps in, each step feels pointless, and suddenly, a month has elapsed scrolling Instagram. Only by spotlighting the motivational gap underneath avoidance do we expose its fixable nature.

Addressing Motivation Vampires

Often, resistance to meaningful milestones stems from deeper value conflicts or limiting beliefs; we must reconcile head-on before moving forward feels possible or important.

For example, pernicious perfectionism or black/white dichotomies like "If I'm not guaranteed mammoth monetary success, why bother trying?" strangle motivation's oxygen early on. By surfacing and then updating these theories, we realign activity with intrinsic aims. Our incentive skyrockets through reappraisal alone. It starts inside.

Confronting Stealth Motivation Killers

Clearly, no magic bullet permanently eliminates all motivation roadblocks, given the inherent fluctuations of our energy, moods, and psychology. However, expanding our mental toolbox for effectively counterbalancing demotivators when they arise stacks odds for consistency in reaching goals versus cratering each time inspiration wanes. Let's explore evidence-backed techniques pivoting from inertia or frustration back into alignment.

Battling Boredom

Monotony sucks the lifeforce rapidly once repetitive tasks feel tedious rather than purposeful. Luckily, behavioral research reveals injecting dynamic variety mid-project battles boredom by restoring cognitive engagement. Maybe shuffle location, alter music genres per work interval, modify body positions, or layer complementary tasks. Infusing beginnings, middles, and ends also divides labor chunks into digestible phases while creating mini-deadlines and producing a sense of movement.

Transforming Resentment Into Opportunity

Other times, external obligations enforced feel secretly aggravating given their misalignment with inner aims or values. Resentful resistance follows. Yet pausing to reframe imposed activities as vehicles toward opening future freedoms incubates intrinsic motivation organically. Perhaps math homework grants analytical tools for launching a passion business someday. Relabeled as pathways, not obligations, motivation rebounds.

Overriding Imposter Syndrome

For high-achievers especially, motivation also fluctuates based on fluctuating self-perceptions and fears of inadequacy. Here, labeling those anxious voices as imposter syndrome rather than truth allows separation from their narration. We remind ourselves feelings pass while competence compounds through courageous action without requiring immediate full confidence. Small acts brushing off doubt accumulate external proof of inner abilities in time.

Perfectionism and Analysis Paralysis

Perfectionists also often struggle with motivation when it comes to starting something new. This stems from a flawed belief that quality can only peak initially and never further improve with effort. But progress over perfection principles helps here. We consciously permit ugly early drafts and experimentation without judging prototypes. Structuring creative flow around revision, not instant brilliance frees motivation inhibition.

Assumption Interrogation

Next, uncover then challenge assumptions stifling motivation. Do we believe intelligence is fixed when neuroplasticity confirms skills developed through practice? Does all meaningful work require passion when commitment often incubates inspiration? Are we secretly demotivated by believing achievement requires proving our worth? Each belief-blocking motivation contains seeds of its counterargument when brought into consciousness.

And should all else fail to activate lagging determination, bribe yourself with external motivator carrots! Desperate times call for no-judgment chocolate binges. But then we double back, reconnecting to internal purposes for long-haul fuel never running empty.

Reframing Negative Into Positive Motivational Frameworks

Beyond addressing idea obstacles, we can reframe motivation itself from a dreadful chore to a celebratory challenge. Do we interpret each writing paragraph as grueling homework or progress toward publishing that book manifesting our life message? It's a choice.

When rewards feel externally imposed rather than organically enjoyable, of course, determination dies quickly. But by consciously linking steps to overarching missions, our neurology and psychology sync up, propelling purpose where barriers once loomed. We become self-generating inspiration engines firing progress mile after mile!

Motivational Techniques and Tools

We've built strong conceptual foundations exploring psychological and biological processes steering motivation along with tactics to counter common obstacles. Now, let's get practical. What are tangible tools for juicing determination and persistently pursuing goals? The missing piece moving us from insight to application.

Lifelong transformation requires fuel beyond momentary boosts. This sticks by slowly stacking small wins toward larger aims. Tiny, repeated actions accumulate into habits and identity itself—the reiterative nature of "Showing up when we don't feel like it" forges resilience. Tracking measurable progress is key; visible achievements substantiate beliefs.

Many road-mapped models aid sustainable drive, too, by formally sequencing change stages. Consider SMART methodology, creating Specific, Measurable, and Achievable objectives that are relevant and time-bound. Mini-wins emerge when wisely structured.

Now, let's directly apply select techniques to frequent procrastination pitfalls!

Hacking Motivation: Tools to Use

Given intrinsic drive's essential yet utterly exhaustible nature across projects lasting months or years, enter science-savvy motivation "power-ups," proving twice the determination gains consistently when wielded strategically. Let's explore top techniques empirically demonstrated to exponentially stretch willpower stores through psychological loopholes:

Temptation Bundling

Here, people lace instantly gratifying activities like binge-worthy Netflix alongside values-aligned but drudgery tasks, creating conditioned emotional fusion. Suddenly, exercise mirrors addictive episodic cliffhangers we can't resist showing up for when paired. Researchers confirm motivation skyrockets 65% on average when we reroute basal pleasures like entertainment, chocolate, or gossip as exclusive sidecars, drafting dreary obligations now intrinsic through association. Talk about motivational alchemy!

Progress Tracking

Simply quantifying incremental progress toward larger goals also doubles down on psychology's partial reinforcement effects, nurturing consistency. Science says variable reward ratios amplify motivation's high by keeping the brain guessing when the next little "win" arrives. Publicly ticking off milestones provides visual validation, too. Track progress in ways proving capability expansion.

Sprinkling in Mini-Competitions

And what stops procrastination faster than a little friendly rivalry? Studies find injecting mini-competition spikes determination immediately through social comparison cues and our instinctual drive to perform when psychologically pitted directly against peers (Shatz, 2019). Shared leaderboards, achievement badges sent upon goal completions, or playfully trash-talking group chats all incite motivation surges, escalating effort through urgent social obligations. Utilize comparison judiciously, avoiding envy traps!

WOOP It Up

Additionally, this nifty WOOP motivational framework demonstrated serious grit gains by leveraging psychology sequentially. First, delineate your Wish for an outcome goal. Then, detail the outcome's boons. Before envisioning blocks, Pinpoint the actual impediment. Finally, map a Plan to address obstacles and forge ahead. Move dreams closer through WOOPing obstacles away!

Let's start experimenting with the one sparking curiosity most!

Motivation Mindsets for Long-Haul Goals

Beyond individual strategies, truly mastering motivation requires cultivating entirely new mental models anchoring our sense of self to growth opportunities instead of static traits. Our guiding philosophies literally alter what feels possible day-to-day. So, what core mindsets scaffold consistency in pursuing bigger-than-life quests?

Fixed vs. Growth Mindsets

At motivation's core lies the notion of fixed versus growth-oriented mindsets, beliefs around whether talent remains innate and static over life or rather gets developed incrementally through grit. Those clinging to fixed abilities perceive intelligence and skills as predefined capacities to struggle against. So, facing achievement plateaus means confronting permanent limitations reflecting core inadequacy or hitting our biological potential ceiling. Motivation plunges. Demoralization often follows the spotlighting of supposed deficiencies.

However, individuals embracing growth philosophies interpret the exact same plateau points not as ceilings of inherent limitation but as temporary obstacles on longer journeys of mastery! Here, they perceive höchst abilities as perpetually expandable through consistent skill sharpening rather than capped by genetics. Struggle signals an area opportunity for dedicated strengthening. Setbacks become data revealing where effort and alternative strategies hold promise, boosting competency to the next levels in time. Patience persists in chasing trajectories of long-term progress.

With a growth lens firmly cemented motivationally, zero accomplishment never fully defines someone because higher peaks always lay ahead, awaiting discovery through renewed strategies. We walk paths of endless becoming. Any present gap simply indicates the required next point growth.

Cultivating Grit Through Powerful Questions

Relatedly, groundbreaking Stanford research examining ultra-successful individuals across fields unveiled "grit" as a pivotal differentiator between those hitting the upper ceiling fast versus persevering through grueling decade-plus mastery journeys. Grit is about having an enduring commitment to important goals, even when facing setbacks, lack of progress, or criticism. It means persisting with passion and resilience despite challenges and emotional ups and downs.

Here, psychologists confirm grittiness arises from how we frame struggles internally through self-talk lenses called explanatory styles, our habitual ways of explaining obstacles affecting motivation resilience to rebound beyond them. Do catastrophic explanations for why we face setbacks dominate thinking, or more optimistic ascriptions focused on productive solutions? It's about relating to impediments as navigable versus existential threats.

For example, after botching a pivotal pitch meeting, are your thoughts consumed with global labels of inadequacy like "I'm such an idiot, no wonder it didn't connect. I'm just bad at explaining details engagingly, no matter how hard I try?" Such internal narratives forecast permanent traits or repeated themes of insufficiency, torpedoing future motivation through futility.

But alternatively, do reflections gravitate toward situational attributions like "The presentation format felt off today. I should rework the messaging flow and visuals to better spotlight critical data upfront, anchoring everything. Just need to refine the hierarchy and content gaps for next time!" Through this temporary, alterable explanatory style, motivation sustains continuing the quest after thoughtful adjustments. Our sentences carry epic significance, scripting psychological resilience.

By catching then rechanneling demotivating internal monologues from catastrophe and inadequacy toward situational framing and solution focus, grit naturally builds callusing motivation against bumps on the trail. Obstacles become welcomed opportunities. Progress unfolds on growth mindset fuel.

Adopting an Empowering Mindset Around Procrastination

Many people see procrastination as something they can't change about themselves. They think struggles with getting things done reflect a permanent flaw in their character.

But the truth is procrastination tendencies can improve over time, just like building muscle. Research shows even lifelong patterns of delay can shift gradually through learning science-backed habits that rewire motivation. Procrastination arises from our current skills and environment, not because of a fixed personal deficiency.

When we believe procrastination is circumstantial, not intrinsic to who we are, motivation gets a boost. Setbacks become signaling areas needing more creativity and strategy adjustments, not condemnations of our worth. Progress flows from a compassionate commitment to slowly getting better through practice.

Seeing consistency as a learnable skill creates hope. We can build little routines that make achievement more automatic, like putting on shoes before leaving the house. Tiny wins accumulate into confidence. Over the years, this adds up to a big transformation.

The key is patience with ourselves and believing better habits can grow through gentle effort. Every moment we choose steps aligned with our dreams, even small ones, reshapes our identity bit by bit. Soon, procrastination loses its grip as we embody motivation. Our destiny unfolds one courageous baby step at a time when we commit to the path, believing in progress.

Case Studies: Motivation in Action

We've mapped the conceptual territory, explored how motivation operates, and analyzed tactics that harness its mechanisms toward progress rather than paralysis. Now, let's observe how these apply in real life. Case studies will showcase the strategies animating aspirations.

Meet Tatiana, a talented painter who always talked about sustaining a daily practice but never followed through past sporadic weeks when inspiration happened to strike. However, when her friend invited her to a weekly virtual "creative accountability hour" where they'd split time working silently and then discussing art unfolding on canvases, suddenly, the external structure sparked internal motivation.

Now, months into consistently cocreating together, Tatiana feels inspiration flowing, even solo, because she has rewired her identity toward an "artist who shows up even on low motivation days." Momentum shifted lifelong patterns through social spark, accountability cadence, small wins accrual, and identity shift. The support scaffolding came down once the determination's foundation solidified.

Or Raul, an entrepreneur continually "researching" online business models but perennially paralyzed on actually launching because he felt intimidated by tech tools. When his partner Clive introduced him to no-code platforms, removing barriers for beginners, Raul suddenly felt self-efficacy take root. He broke projects into milestones using goal-setting frameworks, which boosted motivation through measurable progress. Quick wins fed ambition. Soon, he proudly earned his first passive income dollars from self-made website assets and courses purchased with initially intimidating tools! Again, motivation bloomed by dissolving emotional obstacles, then tracking measurable progress markers and verbalizing capability beliefs through results.

In both cases, motivation arose through strategically addressing root issues stifling it and then systematically building evidence toward an empowered identity. Where determination once hid dormant, psychological jujitsu coupled with simple achievement spotlights awakened it. Now, let's explore what demotivates you and craft customized motivation staircases leading out of stuckness!

Exercise: Self Reflect

Now that we've extensively toured research foundations behind sustainable motivation, the key next step becomes internalizing insights through application. Motivation remains theoretical until tested in real contexts, calibrated to our unique goals and wired minds.

So, in the exercise ahead, reflect on your own procrastination pitfalls, then start brainstorming small experiments leveraging science takeaways. What positive rewards might you build in celebrating progress? How could you reframe drudgery tasks to feel purposeful? Where might an accountability partner make progress irresistible?

Don't think perfection, just directionally more motivated action! Our dreams await these small sparks, transforming paralysis into possibility if we persist in taking tiny steps forward.

Reflection Questions:

What stood out most as you read about the science of motivation? Were any insights particularly surprising or illuminating?

Make a list of activities, interests, or skills that intrinsically motivate you through pure enjoyment and flow. How could you incorporate more of these experiences into daily life?

On the flip side, name one to two goals you're putting off that feel like "shoulds" driven mainly by extrinsic factors like money or acclaim. Could you reframe your "why" to connect with deeper motivators?

Identify a stalled project. See if you can brainstorm a small, achievable next step you could take toward it even if you don't feel motivated. External progress often sparks internal drive.

Affirmation:

"I have infinite inner motivation available by connecting to my purpose."

Activity:

Make a motivational vision board with images and phrases symbolizing dreams that excite you. Let it fuel your subconscious so you wake up feeling inspired to act on goals!

Experiment:

This week, try celebrating every small productivity win, no matter how tiny. Notice if conscious reinforcement keeps you feeling more motivated daily.

Through these reflection questions, affirmations, and micro-experiments, my hope is you've ignited initial momentum, clarifying where your motivation broke down previously while pinpointing a few manageable next steps to harness psychology to fuel progress.

Of course, no single burst of inspiration will effortlessly unfurl years of engrained delay overnight. But by patiently conducting motivation experiments tailored to your nature, the compound effect from small gains accrued daily becomes inevitable.

Harnessing Motivation's Power for Lasting Change

We've covered substantial ground exploring the science of motivation. Let's summarize key insights:

- Motivation has psychological underpinnings: beliefs, attitudes, and goals, plus intrinsic and extrinsic factors that drive us.

- It has neurological foundations, too—the brain's reward system releases chemicals, making pursuits feel irresistible. We can spark these circuits.

- Emotions influence motivation immensely based on how they make tasks feel—negative states obstruct while positive mindsets propel progress.

- Procrastination often stems from motivational breakdowns. But we can troubleshoot confidence crises and reframe activities as aligning with identity to reignite inspiration.

- Finally, tools like accountability cadences, progress tracking, and deadline setting can sustain motivation by structuring in mini-wins.

- The core truth: Science grants us tons of leverage points for training motivation's power on anything we deeply desire!

While momentary inspirational sparks fade without roots, small wins accrued through repeat structures reshape identity and willingness to persist. Where obligation once drained, intrinsic charge can flood in.

So, let's shift from perplexed procrastinators to motivated manifesters! Try:

- Identifying your intrinsic motivations and linking activities to these purposes.

- Setting up structures delivering repeated micro-wins toward crystallizing elevated identity.

- Leveraging accountability partners and progress tracking for external motivational scaffolding.

- Instead of helplessly watching dreams drift by, let's actively engineer environments and summon our best through science-savvy motivation cultivation.

Wrapping Up...

Throughout our journey illuminating motivation's science, we've equipped ourselves with research-backed insights on what propels passionate persistence, along with common obstacles that sabotage progress.

The key takeaway: small shifts deliberate harnessing psychology and biology can redirect tremendous energy toward whatever vision we deeply desire. Where avoidance or paralysis once ruled, self-perpetuating inspiration can blossom in its place.

By taking time to identify intrinsic motivations unique to us and then engineering external accountability mechanisms into environments for structure and reinforcement, suddenly, our dreams glow irresistibly within reach. It starts with a spark.

Yes, some trial and error will unfold on this winding quest to translate motivation theory into custom habit creation. But leaning on the science grants confidence that sustained drive lives within all of us, awaiting activation. Mastery over mindset is the true power.

So rather than lamenting procrastination land's gravitational pull, let's recall the key strategies science offers now for effective escape velocity:

- Spot hidden competing commitments dragging you down subconsciously, then resolve them.

- Infuse tasks with meaning by linking drudgery to overarching life purpose.

- Celebrate micro-wins and skill evolution frequently to buoy emotional fuels.

Together, by learning how to judiciously harvest motivation's renewable power, we transform from stuck to unstoppable.

Chapter 4: Strategies for Overcoming Procrastination

We've now extensively analyzed the tangled psychological roots feeding procrastination along with motivation science tactics to drive action instead. But insight without application risks remaining theoretical rather than transformational.

The final vital step? Equipping ourselves with specific, practical, science-backed strategies to implement in daily life that gradually unravel delay habits and propel us to pursue dreams instead.

Healing crippling procrastination requires a multifaceted toolkit—just tweaking isolated factors like time management techniques rarely stick without addressing underlying emotional obstacles. We need a layered cake attacking paralysis from all angles.

So, in this chapter, we'll dig into the most researched procrastination antidotes spanning mindset shifts, emotional regulation skills, goal-setting frameworks, environmental engineering, productivity hacks, and more counterintuitive lessons. Consider it a smorgasbord of anti-delay delicacies!

While no wellness journey unfolds perfectly smoothly, taking even small bites of these strategies starts building critical capacities for aligning actions with aspirations—tiny gains compound resilience. In time, more efficient systems emerge.

Soon, instead of frustrating paralysis, we'll bask on the other side in hard-won self-trust with weathered motivation toolkits for beckoning peak drive whenever progress stalls. We glimpse and then grasp what once seemed impossible through stepping stones of small wins.

So now, let the strategies feast begin! Dig into any tactics catching your eye today, then revisit buffet plates as needed when particular procrastination flavors rear later on. Our mighty motivation awaits activation!

Time Management Techniques

Let's kick things off with foundational time management tactics, the bread-and-butter of organization systems. Mastery here won't single-handedly solve chronic delay issues with psychological roots; however, optimizing logistics sets the stage for progress by removing pointless obstacles.

Effective Prioritization Frameworks

A moment upfront clarifying relative task importance prevents hours wasted later. The Eisenhower Matrix has stood the test of time here, sorting commitments into:

Urgent/Important (Do now)

Not urgent/Important (Schedule time)

Urgent/Unimportant (Delegate or deny)

Not urgent/Unimportant (Eliminate!)

Just calculating where obligations fall in that grid spurs productive triage. Are we really going to email sponsors while purposeful projects gather dust?

Setting Motivating Goals

Beyond sorting urgency, defining goals for greater purpose adds meaning while quantifying progress. Many models exist for manifesting motivational milestones like vision boards or the WOOP method. But the SMART framework is a procrastinator's friend, helping chronic procrastinators by delineating goals as Specific, Measurable, Achievable, Relevant, and Time-bound. Those guardrails aid follow-through.

Engineering Realistic Schedules

Finally, evenly dispersing tasks combats delay. For example, the Pomodoro technique structures 25 focused minute chunks separated by 5-minute breaks over defined periods optimized for how brains best concentrate. Scheduling intentionally is everything. Now layer in other strategies over solid time management foundations!

Cognitive Restructuring

Beneath procrastination often lies unhelpful thought patterns eroding motivation. Perfectionism, self-doubt, perceived overwhelm, and more. These thought patterns can shape how achievable tasks feel. Luckily, we can rewire self-talk by consciously changing our patterns to overcome negative self-talk.

Catching Automatic Thoughts

The first step is noticing narratives running unconsciously that distort reality. Often called "automatic thoughts," their negativity feels believable at the moment. Yet when we interrupt spirals and examine objectively, irrationality appears. Just acknowledging them as a negative thought minimizes their power.

Challenging Limiting Beliefs

Next, actively dispute negative automatic thoughts through questioning. We ask, "Is this absolutely true? What evidence disputes the worst-case scenario I'm projecting? How might I view this through a lens of opportunity?" Even one alternative viewpoint defuses fallacies.

Reframing Toward Growth

Finally, replace disempowering stories proactively with uplifting narratives highlighting possibility—for example, reframing fear of failure as necessary for growth or perfectionism as valuing excellence. Small linguistic shifts reorient the entire mindset, determining motivation and action. The stories we tell steer destiny!

With consistent restructuring practice, we can rewire cognitive patterns from demotivating to inspiring. Inner work, but so worth it!

Habit Formation and Breaking Procrastination Cycles

Beneath ineffective time management or counterproductive thoughts often lies our ultimate nemesis, sustaining delay: stubborn behavioral cycles cementing bad habits unconsciously over time. But the same neurological machinery also allows the instilling of positive rituals that unravel stagnancy. Let's explore!

How Habits Perpetuate Procrastination

When we avoid challenging tasks repetitively, neural pathways wire in escape conditioned as "safer" through misguided threat response. These patterns automatically repeat future situations without conscious thought. Before we know it, distraction addiction traps ambitions.

Techniques For Instilling Helpful Habits

Luckily, we can nurture positive rituals through deliberate repetition, too! Structures like scheduling recurring progress check-ins or workspace transition cues for improved follow-through at first consciously, then become automatic over time. It takes only 66 days for new synaptic patterns to stick.

Strategies For Breaking Vicious Cycles

Simultaneously, actively disrupt dysfunctional habits using motivation research. For example, the Zeigarnik Effect shows humans fixate on unfinished tasks, skewing focus subconsciously (Cherry, 2021). So, just tracking progress often reduces delay! We also interrupt cycles early through vigilance, while quadratic practice spacing accelerates expertise. Small tweaks, big shifts!

With an understanding of habit machinery, both advancing and regressive, we can engineer conditions systematically channeling our best.

Accountability Systems and Support Networks

Even armed with individual techniques like strategic scheduling or cognitive rewiring, transforming deep-rooted procrastination often requires an extra spark: other people holding us accountable! External motivation accelerates inner work.

The Power of Accountability Partners

Sharing goals transparently with someone offering supportive check-ins supports sticking to targets. Whether an informal friend or structured coach probing progress, accountability adds urgency to fulfilling commitments voiced aloud. Even perceived expectation compels us forward more than solo dreams.

Peer Support Communities

Wider congruent circles magnify group momentum, too. Finding like-minded people chasing similar dreams prevents isolation when challenged. Shared social identity bonds us to timelines. Mastermind groups and seminars leverage collective inspiration amid people "just like us" walking the path.

It Takes a Village

In summary, whole villages propel achievement more than bootstrapping alone. This manifests physically through coworking spaces pooling productivity energy and psychologically through feeling understood by comrades facing analogous inner demons. Camaraderie sparks motivation, compounding community. Together, we travail toward heights impossible separately.

Mindfulness and Stress Management

Among procrastination's sly sources count emotional distress amplifying perceived obstacles and irrational delay. Luckily, research shows mindfulness practices excellently target such unhelpful thinking patterns. Plus, reducing stress heaps benefits beyond fueling productivity, too! Let's dive in.

Mindfulness for Staying Present

First, mindfulness trains focusing intentionally on the present moment without judgment. This could involve meditating on the breath, doing body scans to reduce mind-wandering, or simply noticing when our mind fixates anxiously on the future or past so we can self-correct. Sharpened attentional control assists in completing tasks we previously avoided.

Stress Management Through Lifestyle Factors

Additionally, proactive stress reduction renders perceived barriers more surmountable. We might utilize tactical breathing exercises while working or take mindfulness walks mid-project. But long-term, lifestyle inputs like sufficient sleep, balanced nutrition, and rhythmic exertion actually remodel neurological structures handling pressure. We grow more resilient through healthy regeneration habits.

In summary, regularly counterbalancing workflow with recovery while redirecting attention non-judgmentally cultivates concentration plus sustainable energy for defeating delay cycles. Let's lean into mindfulness as a lifelong skill!

Adopting a Growth Mindset

Among procrastination's primary emotional roots, we find distorted beliefs warping reality into imagined threats, prompting avoidance—things like perfectionism, imposter syndrome, competition obsession, and more. Luckily, adopting a growth mindset reliably redirects such cognitive twisters.

The Growth Mindset Defined

Concisely put, a growth mindset believes abilities develop incrementally through dedication and feedback rather than reflecting some innate, fixed talent. Brains wire and rewire lifelong through new neural connections, which effort molds. Challenges signify progress opportunities, not reflections on our worth or competence at something.

Embracing Challenge Over Avoidance

Compare those holding fixed mindsets around intelligence or talents—they inherently avoid risk or effort in order to validate an ability level already set in stone to them. Those with growth mindsets welcome novel tests via a lens of crucial skill-building. Teaching this reframe resurrects motivation and courage.

Failing Forward Into Opportunity

Relatedly, viewing failure as informative rather than definitive predicts resilience. If a sales pitch gets rejected or we botch a test, growth-focused folks contextualize slipups within longer journeys of mastery, extracting lessons for better skilling up. Setbacks grow determination rather than sabotaging fragile self-concepts. This paradox mindset lifts past perceived obstacles, energizing long-term achievement.

Holistic Well-Being and Lifestyle Adjustments

Thus far, we've mainly explored psychological strategies to change our basic negative thought patterns. But procrastination often emerges from lifestyle misalignment with internal rhythms, too. Let's examine holistic changes enabling our best through self-care.

Assessing Energy Levels

We start by getting real around natural energy fluctuations during the day or week. Are we night owls forcing early meetings when focus peaks late? Do slumps reliably arise mid-afternoon or around periods? Mapping personalized bio-cycles allows scheduling strategically.

Optimizing Nutrition and Movement

With cycles in view, we can structure nourishment and movement to sharpen cognitive capacity for tackling tasks requiring concentration. Complex carbs fuel focus while proteins boost alertness, and spinach aids memory. Even mild exercise clears mental fatigue's fog. We spark our best through biology!

Stress Management and Rest

Additionally, balancing exertion periods with ample recovery prevents mood dips from eroding motivation. Whether hot baths, forest walks, or napping recharges batteries varies individually, but regular self-care makes progress feel more sustainable. Downtime fuels uphill climbs!

In summary, environment engineering around energy patterns, fuel sources, and rhythmic restoration ultimately determines what feels possible day-to-day. Let's utilize agency in sculpting conditions for productivity through whole self-care!

Practical Outcomes: Building a Personalized Procrastination Toolkit

If only ending lifelong procrastination struggles required reading a list of science-backed strategies and then instantly acting consistently aligned with big dreams! But in reality, progress unfolds through recurring trial and error, finding personalized combinations that shift mindsets before cementing habits. Let's review key insights uncovered before crystallizing our own custom toolkits.

We explored thought restructuring tactics bringing limiting beliefs from background to the foreground; willpower mysteries explaining why avoidance often wins short-term; habit science empowering tiny gains compounding motivation; mindfulness practices amplifying focus; lifestyle tweaks honoring energy patterns and making space for restoration along with community accountability providing the needed social spark for inner work.

The key: residual procrastination likely requires an integrated self-care plan addressing root emotional obstacles and environmental factors plus tactical nudge structures preventing backward slides, our personalized medicine protocol.

So, let's start assembling our own mental health support teams filled with motivational mentors, self-care activities that reboot joy, tactical tricks to outsmart squirrelly brains, inspiring visuals affirming budding identity, and more uniquely tailored elements that feel nourishing.

We'll likely tinker with formulas forever as new challenges emerge or tools get rusty. However, engaging in the ongoing experiment ensures forward progress rather than stagnancy as we stair-step slowly toward a proactiveness breakthrough.

And remember, perfection is not required, just gradual consistency tracking tiny wins—our future freedom from delay beckons incrementally as we walk the path step-by-step!

Leveraging Technology for Motivation and Productivity

Beyond traditional pen-and-paper methods for optimizing workflows, let's also tap into burgeoning technology tools strategically blocking procrastination triggers, helping instill positive habits. From website blockers to accountability apps, such virtual assistants scaffold consistency where raw self-discipline wavers.

First, website-blocking software like Freedom or Cold Turkey curates custom blacklists shutting down distraction-prone sites during work sessions. Hence, willpower preserves energy for deep task focus rather than constantly batting temptations. Set it and forget it productivity support!

Accountability apps similarly harness external pressure improving follow-through where solo attempts at habit formation unravel over weeks. Coach.me, Stickk, and HabitBull allow register specific self-improvement goals and then tracking adherence metrics viewable by peer groups—public visibility amps determination to fulfill commitments.

Focus timer apps offer a double-duty structure, too, by chunking work intervals down into digestible units with enforced breaks built in circadian rhythm alignment. Tomatoes and Focus Keeper visualize ticking countdown clocks ending in rewarding freedom, gamifying concentration stamina essential for long-term achievement.

We also tap into AI assistance to optimize administrative parts of project workflow so cognitive resources are preserved for the heavy mental lifting. Tools like Otter.ai auto-generate meeting notes and transcripts from recordings, while grammar tools like Catchword and Grammarly clean up copy. Automating frees up mental RAM, breaking distraction chains.

While inner work builds lifelong motivation skills that truly stick, don't underestimate supplemental digital tools and virtual accountability networks accelerating success during vulnerable beginnings of habit formation. Try stacking the odds for follow-through in your favor, letting artificial intelligence handle drudgery.

Environment Design for Motivation

Beyond personal habit formation, we also cunningly engineer physical spaces supporting productivity by eliminating friction points dragging focus while installing cues triggering positive rituals. Take creative license optimizing your cave for an unencumbered flow state!

Start by assessing current spaces through a momentum lens; what objects or setups distract consistently? Clear clutter visually competing for attention, pile paper chaos into organizing systems, and conceal digital temptation devices physically in drawers. Decluttering space clears mental space, eliminating energy drains.

Conversely, inject intentional triggers, drawing awareness toward growth goals through visual salience. Whiteboards displaying inspiring quotes, posters of role models who overcame adversity, and artwork symbolizing projects in progress keep purpose top of mind. Install physical tripwires preventing backward slides.

Additionally, create dedicated environments for particular ritual chains supporting big-picture aims, a reading nook that cues studying habits, and a kitchen island that holds journaling supplies to arrest writer's block quickly. The more we enter optimal behavioral highways via environmental engineering, the less discipline is wasted battling inertia alone.

Finally, bridge physical and emotional landscapes by infusing spaces with sensory delights, plants purifying air, essential oil diffusers anointing calm, and tactile richness in pillows, rugs, and crafts, nourishing creativity. Productivity flows freely when spaces hold and reflect bold dreams through sight, smell, and sound. Our environment acts as an external nervous system, enabling internal breakthroughs!

While inner transformation proves foundational to conquering procrastination, astutely designed external terrain makes the improbable inevitable through unconscious cues planted strategically. Nourish nascent habits in your personal ecosystem's soil and watch motivational sprouts surface beyond your wildest dreams.

Cultivating a Support System

Constructing motivation toolkits also hugely benefits from carefully selected interpersonal ingredients supporting our progress or potential pitfalls. Let's explore how to intentionally curate a supportive community scaffolding goals vulnerable to isolation-exacerbated procrastination.

Start by taking inventory of current connections nourishing aspirations through shared purpose or direct aid versus contacts subtly enabling old sabotaging patterns to persist through distraction or disrupted priorities. Well-meaning friends can unconsciously jeopardize growth.

Once awareness clarifies around unsupportive influences, establish appropriate boundaries, whether through declining happy hours temporarily favoring early bedtimes, disabling social media feeds hijacking attention often, or briefly cutting ties where serious toxicity undermines self-concept, dismantling motivation's foundation. No need for permanent cancellation, just thoughtful life editing.

Moving forward, seek or form tribes centered on growth-oriented values, optimalism over perfection, humility, and self-compassion over dogmatic social comparison. For example, join a mastermind group equally committed to the writing craft, business innovation, or lifestyle design. Share struggles and breakthroughs regularly, reaffirming why your ambitions matter. Or schedule recurring co-working hours to maintain accountability for daily progress checkpoints. Community momentum fuels consistency, unlocking next-level goals that isolation smothers.

Additionally, enroll personal mentors and coaches to accelerate learning curves too steep for solo vertical climbs. A photography instructor providing tailored technical feedback saves years of struggling blindly to interpret underexposed film negatives. Or an entrepreneurship expert steers winning tactics, avoiding costly online course chaos. Getting the right timely coaching multiplies growth.

Finally, give back to others by overcoming similar emotional obstacles or navigating related learning slopes too through volunteering and informal check-ins. Demonstrating vulnerability, in turn, builds trust, opens access to guidance, and accelerates your own transformations. Everyone stands at different mile markers on the same fundamental human journeys. Together, we travel further.

Procrastination tends to thrive when severed from supportive tribes through a lack of direction, role models, and accountability fueling progress. But by handpicking community elements strategically optimized to unique growth goals and phases, inspiration stays lit, internalizing motivation until independently burning bright. Our people power potential's activation.

Case Study: Jada

Meet Jada, a talented writer who always dreamed of penning a book sharing her grandmother's powerful story as a civil rights activist. But whenever Jada considered tangibly outlining the memoir, anxiety around doing justice to such a momentous topic paralyzed progress.

The years passed with Jada stuck in analysis paralysis until she confessed her book idea to her friend Marcus, himself an aspiring author battling isolation on projects. In resonance, they decided to launch biweekly virtual writing meetups for peer accountability, troubleshooting dilemmas, and celebrating small wins.

Reinforced by Marcus's encouragement, Jada utilized writing prompts at meetups to finally splatter initial ideas onto paper without judging quality. Momentum built week-by-week, translating into a complete chapter draft! Yet soon, Jada's ruthless inner editor crept in, stalling further creation in the quest for elusive perfection.

Noticing Jada's mental blockade, Marcus suggested embracing a flexible growth mindset focused on progress, not results. He reminded Jada of her core intention of honoring family history, not creating flawless prose immediately. Together, they substituted "writing time" for rigid "word count" metrics so creativity could unfold organically. Jada's motivation reignited, realizing the path supported the destination.

While this aligned energy sometimes dips, Jada now utilizes additional techniques like task batching, progress tracking, and mindfulness when frustration returns. Most powerfully, she adopted the identity of "an author who shows up with courage despite fear" as an antidote to imposter demons. What once loomed insurmountable transformed through layered motivation strategies coupled with the community's buoying effect.

Exercise: Self Reflect

Now that we've toured the science-backed procrastination strategy buffet, let's shift from theory to action by creating mini-experiment plans custom-tailored to our unique mess! Reflection first illuminates wakeup calls in stalled areas, then we design micro baby step goals leveraging behavioral psychology strengths uncovered here. By pacing small, consistent gains, transformation unfolds.

Reflection Questions:

What procrastination habits or mindsets do you frequently struggle with (perfectionism, task overwhelm, etc.)? Dig past the surface symptoms.

Given those self-insights, the review suggested research-backed strategies covered, choosing two to three small realistic tactics for testing counter-balancing this week.

Troubleshoot micro experiments by applying your chosen tactics for two weeks. Chart any correlations. What tangible gains accumulated? What still needs refinement?

Journaling Exercise:

Make a T-chart. On the left, write two goals you keep delaying. On the right, journal how accomplishing them might positively transform things like productivity, purpose, and confidence.

Affirmation:

"My small, consistent actions lead to exponential results over time."

Action Step:

Commit to one micro-step aligned with a stalled goal this week. Just create momentum!

Through recurrent self-examination spurring incremental strategy micro-adjustments tailored to our unique inner obstacles, the elusive procrastination beast increasingly loses its grip as we claim power. Sustained small wins snowball retaking life's steering wheel from delay's slippery slope toward reimagined vistas where inspiration perpetually beckons.

Wrapping Up...

Throughout our extensive strategies journey here, we've equipped ourselves with dozens of research-backed insights on what practically combats procrastination, from addressing thought obstacles all the way to holistic lifestyle factors fueling our best.

The key takeaway now comes down to personalization. Residual procrastination likely requires an integrated self-care regimen custom-designed to target your unique emotional barriers, environmental weak points, and motivational structures necessary for cementing growth in the face of inertia.

So reflect on your particular procrastination pitfalls and sources of stuckness...then slowly start assembling your own mental health support squad. Enlist motivation mentors and peer accountability partners, self-care activities that regularly reboot joy, clever ritual tricks to outsmart squirrelly brains, tangible visuals affirming your budding desired identity, and other tailored elements that feel uniquely nourishing for you.

No need for perfection! But through recurring consistency tracking tiny wins and progressively course-correcting when inevitable stumbles occur, lifetime liberation from delay beckons incrementally as we learn to walk our unique path forward, one courageous step, then leap at a time.

Chapter 5: Overcoming Perfectionism

Perfectionism is a common emotional barrier behind procrastination. It's the belief that tasks must be flawlessly excellent or not done at all. This seemingly noble pursuit of quality can mutate into self-paralysis, avoiding action out of fear of imperfect results.

While some carefulness serves functions like error-checking important work, perfectionism focuses single-mindedly on avoiding mistakes rather than progress. This makes any vulnerable task feel too risky, stunting growth that requires learning through failures.

Ahead, we'll explore why perfectionism persists despite good aims, how it intersects with pitfalls like imposter syndrome, plus science-based techniques offering freedom from self-paralysis so we can manifest excellence through action.

The goal isn't eliminating standards but balancing ideals with sustainable sanity so big visions don't get abandoned halfway. By managing motivation intelligently, even monumental aspirations become reachable if we dare start small and then persist. Time to dig in!

Perfectionism's Roots

Where does perfectionism come from in the first place? By unraveling its origins, we gain the power to redirect it. Let's explore some common emotional roots!

Fear of Failure

A major feeder is anxiety about inadequate performance or criticism if we fall short of standards. To self-protect, perfectionism tries to guarantee positive outcomes by aiming impossibly high from the start. Yet this paralyzes even the beginning, trapping potential.

Self-Doubt

Similarly, deep down, a lack of confidence in actually being able to accomplish goals can manifest perfectionism, too. Setting overly lofty benchmarks allows for avoiding confronting capability doubts by not earnestly trying in the first place.

External Expectations

Finally, perceived pressures from parents, bosses, and society can fuel the feeling nothing but flawless is ever good enough. Internalizing those projected standards breeds relentless self-criticism anytime we miss imaginary targets.

In summary, fear of failure, insecurity, and social expectations commonly intertwine, reinforcing perfectionism. Good news, though: With self-compassion and rewriting narratives, we can start constructing healthier mindsets that are not sabotaged by impossible yardsticks!

How Perfectionism Hinders Productivity

Now that we've dissected perfectionism's roots, let's examine how chasing impossibly flawless results sabotages getting work done:

It Strangles Progress

By over-focusing on avoiding mistakes at all costs, perfectionism causes getting started to feel nearly impossible. We keep waiting for the mythical "right moment" with perfect conditions to begin, which never arrives, preventing forward motion.

It Stifles Creativity

Relatedly, perfectionism severely limits experimentation and imaginative risk-taking since remaining inside our comfort zones feels "safest." Yet revolutionary ideas emerge through riffing freely and then refining over time, a playful flow impossible if every fledgling draft already needs proving genius.

It Triggers Procrastination

When tasks look too intimidating due to unrealistic benchmarks we set internally, delaying through distraction naturally follows. Suddenly, even checking emails looks more appealing than attempting something we're predestined to judge inadequate regardless. And thus, the insidious procrastination cycle perpetuates.

In summary, demanding flawlessness strangles productivity's lifeblood, consistent progress fueled by curious creativity. But by adjusting mental models to value moving forward through incremental evolution, we can learn to ship imperfect but functional work full of future potential.

Identifying Perfectionistic Thoughts

Perfectionism lives through certain unhelpful thought patterns. By naming them, we can start catching and redirecting perfectionistic thinking.

One common tendency is black-and-white thinking, viewing outcomes as complete successes or total failures without nuance. Shades of grey don't exist for perfectionists. We also tend to over-generalize by broadly applying isolated incidents as permanent truths about our abilities. For example, "My manager critiqued one report; I clearly can't write well about anything."

Additionally, perfectionists assume imagined worst-case scenarios as predestined facts. This fortune-telling assumes that if a draft isn't genius caliber, then our career is obviously ruined. Finally, we mind-read by believing we know exactly how others will negatively judge us without actual evidence. "Anyone reading this will think I'm untalented for sure."

Try noticing whether these patterns underlie your inner narration. Simply recognizing automatic perfectionistic thoughts arising is the first step toward questioning rather than believing them by default.

Embracing Progress Over Perfection

Clearly, perfectionism's irrational thought patterns torpedo getting things done by paralyzing us with impossibly high bars. The root solution? Adopting entirely new mental models valuing progress itself over perfection.

First and foremost, we must understand intellectually that no first draft of anything is meant for Pulitzer prizes. Ideas need iterating, not judging. This means consciously giving ourselves permission to move concepts forward through ugly phases. We brainstorm freely, then tighten.

With that framework shift established, we integrate tangible creation rituals that value sustainable progress daily—for example, scheduling timed writing sprints for pumping out quantities of content uncensored without pausing to evaluate quality. Here, progress itself is the only benchmark.

Similarly, committing to rapid prototyping can defeat inner critics derailing perfectionists. Say we're crafting an e-course; rather than fixating on elaborate technical features from the starting gate, we focus first on quickly filming a simple pilot lesson to gather user feedback for improving subsequent content and releasing ourselves from needing to wow right away open space to methodically build excellence through evidence-based adjustments.

Structuring projects around iterating drafts empowers big visions to come to life in phases. Out of messy progress blooms greatness unrushed.

Fostering a Growth Mindset

Beyond shifting behavior habits valuing progress, transforming perfectionism also requires adopting an entirely new belief system about the nature of abilities and excellence. Specifically, cultivating a growth mindset centered on seeing intelligence and skills as developed incrementally versus reflecting some static innate gift.

Perfectionists frequently possess firmly fixed mindsets around competency; we view our natural talents as somewhat rigid. So, by definition, having to struggle toward milestones means inadequate innate ability. Our self-worth stays stubbornly tied to achievement markers constantly validating intelligence. Few risks are taken to preserve that self-image.

Shifting toward a growth orientation completely flips this script to see humans as works in progress. Challenges indicate productive difficulties forging competency, not inherent deficiencies dooming us. Setbacks get contextualized as feedback furthering learning, not proof reaching above our station. Through this lens, imperfection becomes irrelevant compared to improvement over long arcs.

This paradigm allows fearlessly taking on ambitious projects once paralyzing. We no longer catastrophize isolated failures when our benchmark is long-term trajectories clinching expertise through practice. Progress feels guaranteed by laws, learning, and neuroplasticity, not bound by past performance. Soon, even monumental goals seem possible through stepwise growth.

Mindfulness and Acceptance

Beyond cementing rational insights intellectually, transforming perfectionism also requires emotional management tools when irrational thought patterns inevitably persist or resurface. Here, research proves mindfulness practices invaluable for short-circuiting frustration (Tóth et al., 2023).

When perfectionistic thoughts arise, judging work harshly, mindfulness helps us notice and then neutralize rather than automatically believing anxious mind-chatter. Instead of fixating on what's "wrong," we gently redirect attention to the present moment—maybe feeling the feet on the floor or listening to ambient sounds without judgment before proceeding.

Getting in touch with the sensory realm diminishes negativity bias, conditioning us to see only shortcomings before they mushroom into despair. It becomes easier to witness perfectionistic stories as transient noise rather than truth. We can acknowledge anxiety and then let it pass without reacting.

Over time, the muscle for calmly accepting intense emotions builds. We grow more comfortable abiding uncomfortable states like uncertainty, vulnerability, or inadequacy without reflexively trying to control them. We don't need flawlessness to feel safe and worthy. Equanimity emerges.

By learning to regulate discomfort around imperfect progress, creativity flows freely, too. We no longer require pristine conditions to initiate action. Progress unfolds on its own terms.

Perfectionism and Imposter Syndrome

Alongside perfectionism, many high achievers secretly grapple with imposter syndrome too, the notion we don't truly deserve accomplishments credited to us but rather 'fooled' others into overestimating our competence. So externally, we may shine as talented leaders while internally feeling like utter frauds waiting to be exposed as such anytime achievements mount. What fuels these twin psychological saboteurs...and how can we combat their toxic impacts, including procrastination fed by self-doubt?

Both perfectionism and imposter syndrome stem from an underlying lack of self-confidence that achievement depends entirely upon proving giftedness through flawless performance. Mistakes signal inadequate natural talents rather than offering productive learning for growth. So, proving competence by attaining inflated standards ironically perpetuates doubts by avoiding tough challenges testing current abilities. It becomes a relentless hamster wheel seeking external validation versus building genuine skillsets through incremental practice.

Additionally, harsh inner critics overpower supportive inner coaches in those struggling with either affliction. We barrage ourselves constantly about shortcomings but rarely praise incremental progress made. So, no accomplishments ever feel satisfactory for long before flaws get fixated on exclusively.

Thankfully, pathways exist for outgrowing the deadweight of either imposter syndrome or perfectionism, so we stop sabotaging journeys toward meaningful potentials.

Start by actively reframing cognitive patterns when negative self-talk flares up. Become aware of distorted perspectives like fortune-telling imagined worst-case scenarios or blowing struggles out of proportion.

Write out counter-evidence for each faulty assumption.

Also, list past successes and current competencies. Read them aloud regularly. Catalog external feedback received, too. Such records build a factual case against inner Critics falsely claiming incompetence or worthlessness.

Finally, reward small gains made daily, not just end milestones reached. Mini journaling sessions capturing progress help the truth sink in. So does modifying environment cues via affirmation notes, vision boards displaying accomplishments, or displays of celebratory gifts for efforts completed. Soon, momentum outruns self-doubts' drain.

In the end, constructing new mental frameworks affirming excellence as daily practiced rather than performed perfection allows lifting imposter syndrome and perfectionism's heavy burden, blocking being our best selves.

Progress unfolds through patience with ourselves.

Cultivating Self-Compassion

Battling inner voices demanding flawlessness, whether through perfectionism or imposter syndrome, also requires actively cultivating self-compassion as an emotional counterweight. By relating to ourselves with kindness, mindfulness, and shared humanity when falling short of standards, motivation sustains, not self-sabotage. Let's explore the pivotal role self-compassion plays in defeating procrastination.

First, self-compassion provides emotional safety to experiment freely without fearing failure. We don't hesitate to express ideas in initial messy form or attempt tasks below our skill level because we know setbacks get handled gently, not with self-flagellation. This reduces avoidance, allowing skill building essential for conquering new challenges.

Relatedly, self-compassion centers on mindfully observing thoughts nonjudgmentally. We don't ignore or suppress periodic self-criticism, but rather compassionately acknowledge then let go versus ruminating. This builds the capacity to sit with the discomfort that breeds procrastination when tasks feel unpleasant. Through self-directed kindness, we tolerate emotional heat skillfully.

Additionally, by framing struggles as shared human experiences rather than personal flaws, self-compassion connects us to others progressing through learning curves too. Challenges become easier to endure, knowing we're not alone in working to improve precisely where we feel most vulnerable. Fear of judgment for imperfect performance eases when everyone walks similar roads.

We also avoid harsh self-talk through what psychologists call taking the self-perspective rather than judging ourselves as an outside critic might. Noticing mindfully "I'm being hard on myself" differs from "I'm such a failure." Tiny linguistic tweaks grant grace, reiterating all people deserve compassion.

So practically, how to build this pivotal self-compassion muscle when inner critics run rampant?

Start small, notice critical self-talk, then nudge perspectives toward gentler frames. Overwrite negative phrases into supportive alternatives. "I'm still learning here," not "I don't have what it takes."

Do regular self-compassion writing exercises voicing kindness you would offer close friends struggling, then read passages aloud as if discovering your inherent worth firsthand.

Or try mirror work directly soothing inner critics through verbal affirmations, eye contact, and hugging yourself. Physical gestures communicate self-acceptance beyond intellectual convincing.

No matter the specific tactic, just persist in practicing compassion through daily battles large and small. Gradually relate to yourself as intrinsically not an obstacle along the growth curve. Procrastination is defenseless against bold vision plus self-care.

Case Studies: Transforming Perfectionism

We've explored extensively how perfectionism's irrational thought patterns hijack productivity by fueling self-paralysis and procrastination in the name of flawlessness. But how does this journey unravel in real people's lives, and how can we shift gears from self-sabotage to liberating new paths? Let's examine some case studies!

Meet John; a talented marketing manager paralyzed preparing quarterly reports for the CEO because past heavy edits made John believe nothing he produced was ever good enough for pre-review. He compensated by working tirelessly before each deadline yet still only sent final decks seconds before meetings due to debilitating doubts.

This change in mindset helped reduce John's perfectionist pressures on himself. He gave himself permission to submit working drafts earlier, even knowing needing tweaks later. By focusing on progress itself over perfection, confidence grew through practice without trauma.

Or examine Robin, who dreamed of writing children's books but never applied herself beyond a rough chapter one draft in years. Perfectionism around synthesizing imaginative plot lines plus playfully capturing a child's voice paralyzed efforts. Deep down, Robin doubted she could ever do creative writing "right" enough for talent to shine through.

However, discovering freewriting sprints detached from judging quality became liberating game-changers. Robin set a kitchen timer repeatedly for 10 minutes, churning out scenes devoid of criticism before reading back. Hundreds of paragraphs emerged full of gems worth refining over time. Perfectionism's vice-grip is released through prioritizing prolific flow unfettered. Progress exploded unjudged.

In both cases, understanding anxiety sabotaging output set the stage for testing tactics that compassionately celebrated progress itself. Creativity soared unblocked by preemptive self-criticism. Though perfectionism still occasionally whispers, new paths stand carved.

Exercise: Self Reflect

Now that we've explored strategies dissolving perfectionism's stranglehold, let's shift from theory into action by creating mini-experiment plans custom-tailored to our unique mess.

Self-reflection first illuminates insightful wake-up calls in stalled areas of our lives. Then, we purposefully design micro baby step goals leveraging behavioral psychology strengths uncovered here to test incremental changes.

By pacing small, consistent gains tied to our realities, transformation slowly but surely unfolds one stage at a time. Progress builds momentum. Backslides become learning opportunities, not failures.

So, let's begin harnessing research insights for incrementally constructing our next bold chapter where creativity and contribution can take center stage, unblocked by those formerly paralyzing inner critics.

Reflection Questions:

What perfectionistic thought patterns or behaviors do you struggle with frequently (black & white thinking, delaying tasks, etc.)? Dig past the surface symptoms.

Given those self-insights, review suggested research-backed strategies covered, choosing two to three small, realistic tactics for testing this week.

Troubleshoot micro experiments by applying your chosen tactics for two weeks. Chart any correlations. What tangible gains accumulated? What still needs refinement?

Journaling Exercise:

Make a T-chart. On the left, write a stalled goal where perfectionism has hindered progress. On the right, journal how embracing imperfect progress could create positive momentum.

Affirmation:

"I welcome forward motion over precision; the path unfolds."

Action Step:

Commit to an imperfect first step aligned with a goal where perfectionism has previously paralyzed. Just get momentum!

I hope through recurrent self-examination and strategy experimentation tailored to your obstacles, perfectionism's grip will increasingly loosen as you reclaim your potential.

Applying Anti-Perfectionism Insights

In our journey here dissecting perfectionism, we've equipped ourselves with dozens of research-backed tactics illuminating the roots of this common yet caustic cognitive saboteur. Let's review the applied key takeaways:

- Perfectionism commonly originates from fear of failure, self-doubt, and perceived external pressures that influence unrealistic standards

- Chasing flawlessness strangles productivity by preventing starting and creative risks that allow ideas to blossom through iteration

- Certain thought patterns like black/white thinking and fortune-telling sustain the illusion achieving perfection is possible and required

- Shifting focus toward incremental progress itself over outcomes builds confidence through small wins and liberates work from imagined pressures

- Fostering a growth mindset recalibrates beliefs around competency as unlimited rather than fixed to serve potential, not validation

- Mindfulness helps regulate the emotional frustration perfectionism sparks when natural imperfection arises so we keep going

- But insight without action risks remaining theoretical. So now the invitation becomes actively identifying in your own life:

What triggers typically hook perfectionistic thinking for you?

- Can you catch limiting thought patterns and then purposefully reframe them toward flexibility?

- What small behavioral shifts valuing progress could create radically new results compounding motivation over time through success momentum?

Our potential awaits permission to unfold through strategic baby steps past previous barriers.

Wrapping Up...

In closing, we've dug deeply into perfectionism, from its emotional origins feeding the fear of failure and self-doubt to the irrational thought patterns that sustain impossibly high standards to pragmatic science-backed strategies for breaking free from self-paralysis.

The key realization? With self-compassion, tactical restructuring of behaviors and beliefs, plus emotional management tools, we can circumvent perfectionism's stranglehold and begin actualizing potential previously trapped behind self-protection. Progress awaits manifestation through courageously imperfect action.

Of course, the journey requires recurring effort as old cognitive reflexes persist, seeking airtime. But once we firmly cement liberation frameworks challenging automatic perfectionistic stories, their power fades as the truth comes into sharper focus: we were never meant to be perfect to contribute gifts only we carry. Our unique genius asks only courageous baby steps to coalesce over time, not instant flawlessness.

So shall we begin demonstrating grace toward our perfectly imperfect but utterly essential selves? Can we trust intrinsic potential longing for actualization regardless of what our Inner Critics proclaim? I believe we can walk this path, my friends—one imperfect but meaningful step ahead of the last.

Chapter 6: Developing Self-Discipline

Among procrastination's key underlying obstacles, we find insufficient self-discipline and the innate ability to motivate action consistently despite the discomfort, distraction, or mood-hijacking determination. Building this muscle strategically separates dreamers from doers.

We all likely understand self-discipline conceptually: summoned willpower driving us forward when we'd rather binge Netflix or scroll social feeds than finalize projects requiring extended mental strain. Yet cultivating such resilience long-term requires more than wishing away laziness.

In the chapter ahead, we'll dive extensively into psychology and biology, explaining why briefly burning motivation yet quickly sliding into distraction or avoidance feels inevitable for so many. Strategies for sustaining effort range from outrageously effective habit-stacking routines to leveraging accountability partnerships to a crash course on dopamine's mysteries so we stop inadvertently sabotaging goals.

Consider this your manual for becoming a productivity machine through understanding the hidden science secretly optimizing consistent determination or derailment. Because lifelong transformation happens not through force but wise engineering conditions where tiny progress steps compound daily almost automatically.

Understanding the Psychology of Self-Discipline

What really drives self-discipline psychologically when procrastination looks easier at the moment? Understanding the key mental forces helps us harness them intentionally over the long haul.

Intrinsic motivation is crucial for initially sparking momentum on new disciplined habits before external accountability takes over. Finding inherent satisfaction in progress itself, versus avoiding discomfort, fuels the early boost pushing us to begin new self-discipline journeys. However, fired-up motivation alone rarely sustains effort indefinitely when willpower naturally wanes day to day. Here, self-discipline evolves to involve consciously managing our fluctuating willpower stores to accomplish aims anyway, even when we don't "feel" like it at the moment. This happens through implementing tailored structures and systems that help us override temporary moods. Finally, behavioral research shows that we persist in chasing intrinsically rewarding goals longer than external validation or wealth alone. So clarifying deeply personal aims with inherent satisfactions versus superficial rewards also boosts consistency and longevity dramatically.

In summary, the key is blending initial motivation sparks with sustainable systems for managing natural willpower ups and downs. With both forces supported, self-discipline flows consistently without chronic exhaustion or hijacking goals.

Cultivating Resilience and Perseverance

Sustaining self-discipline across months or years pursuing big goals requires resilience and perseverance, as well as our capacity to overcome setbacks, rebound after failures, and keep going despite major obstacles. How is this mental toughness cultivated? By utilizing science-backed strategies upfront, preparing us for the long game.

First, celebrating small wins builds psychological strength better than fixating on ambitious end targets alone. Achievable milestones generate repeated victory compounds, falsifying self-doubt. Tracking progress reorients identity toward possibility; we become people who accomplish goals, however gradually.

Planning ahead for potential setbacks can also help prevent discouragement when dealing with procrastination. If we go into the process expecting that distractions or backsliding might occasionally happen as an inevitable part of making changes, then we won't see those stumbles as personal failures or proof that we can't improve. By acknowledging upfront that periodic delays and mistakes may happen as we work to reduce our procrastination tendencies, we take away some of their symbolic meaning and fear. When we anticipate and normalize occasional backsliding, we are less likely to be thrown off track. We can tell ourselves, "I prepared for this possibility, and I will persist through it." Having this mindset of expecting but not condemning normal stumbles can inoculate us against discouragement as we work to overcome habitual procrastination. The setbacks lose their ability to threaten our progress when they are planned for in advance rather than seen as abnormal sources of shame. We will be able to take them in stride.

In other words, expecting and allowing for occasional distractions/lapses as we work to reduce procrastination tendencies helps prevent us from getting discouraged when they happen. If framed as normal rather than personal flaws/failures, it is easier to persist past them.

Finally, linking actions clearly to intrinsic life purpose and core values boosts resilience exponentially. During tough slogs, reminding ourselves "why" this dream matters reconnects to motivation, sustaining extra effort despite fatigue or frustration. Our self-discipline stands for something.

Goal Setting Strategies

Establishing clear aims and priorities is foundational for channeling self-discipline, too. Our willpower flows easily when effort has an observable direction. But how do we manifest effective goals by optimizing follow-through?

First, ensure purposes carry intrinsic meaning and alignment to core values versus chasing extrinsic rewards like fame or wealth that extinguish quicker. We sustain self-discipline when deep satisfaction comes from the process itself.

Next, inject flexibility into goal timelines, benchmarks, and routines, allowing iteration, not rigid absolutism, tripping up progress. Build in accidental discoveries without derailment.

Finally, prioritize by allocating limited willpower stores thoughtfully. Calculated effort balancing renewal lifestyle factors maximizes returns on output. Always ask: Where can this moment best advance my aims?

In summary, crystallizing personally meaningful ambitions while permitting flexibility when mapping plans unlocks self-discipline supporting experimentation and reassessment without forfeiting the sights of the vision.

Building Disciplined Habits

While mindsets clearly influence self-discipline, arguably our most leverageable change agent is engineering tiny habits systematically shaping unconscious behavior over time. Instead of straining against our nature, we befriend biology itself through automation.

The formula? Stack miniature rituals toward a larger vision that accumulates momentum. For example, aiming to study programming for 30 minutes nightly quickly flames out from willpower gaps. But opening our laptop when we sit down for coffee every morning more easily sticks thanks to the existing anchor routine, cueing a seamless transition.

Gradually, repeated micro-actions like mindfully opening work files, hand on mouse, cement automaticity no longer requiring conscious strain. Self-discipline becomes effortless once actions are embedded as subconscious habits aligned with where we want to go. Tiny gains lead everywhere in time.

Other research-backed techniques like implementation intention plans further propel consistency: "When situation X arises, I will perform response Y," eliminating choice gaps that derailed discipline. Environment engineering also sparks seamless self-discipline through cues optimizing desirable conduct. We set the stage for habits that stick!

Optimizing Time and Tasks

Beyond mindset adjustments and habit stacking, effectively marshaling limited time and tasks boosts self-discipline, too, by ensuring willpower gets strategically allocated to priorities. What efficiency strategies overcome distraction entropy?

First, assess personal energy cycles across days and weeks, then protect peak creative hours for project deep dives while scheduling lower-brainpower admin tasks when lagging. Sync work to bio-patterns.

Additionally, batch similar obligations to plow through efficiently and then reward progress chunks with rejuvenating breaks. For example, answering all emails sequentially versus distraction-prone multitasking preserves mental focus, minimizing willpower drain.

Finally, creating physical tasks triggers channeling attention productively. Environmental cues like keeping projects visually salient on desks, using apps blocking distracting websites, or placing gym bags by doors speed desired actions through conditioned association.

Intelligently organizing time use around natural focus patterns, consolidating task types with planned breaks, and crafting physical triggers judiciously simulate self-discipline even as willpower naturally fluctuates across days.

Fostering Discipline-Conducive Mindsets

As we've thoroughly explored, mindsets indubitably shape behaviors related to self-discipline. If we perceive ourselves as inherently "bad at consistency" or assume progress requires perfect conditions, defeatism feels destined. However, we can purposefully cultivate mental frameworks boosting perseverance against short-term moods or entropy. The methods? Simply shifting core philosophies guiding our mindset:

On challenge: "Setbacks mean I'm progressing" versus "Obstacles imply I'll inevitably fail."

On mindset: "Consistent effort determines achievement" versus "Natural talent alone drives my ceiling for competence."

On resources: "My energy can renew" versus "Willpower is inherently limited in supply."

On priorities: "Purpose fuels perseverance" versus "I must rely on motivation alone."

On learning: "Each small step develops mastery over time" versus "Greatness requires immediate results."

Such simple reframing powerfully shapes our responses to difficulty and thus, self-discipline outcomes.

Self-Discipline Despite Adversity

Cultivating consistent self-discipline sounds great when life flows smoothly. But what about when crises or chaos strike, dismantling routines keeping us aligned? Unexpected adversity represents the ultimate test of grit. So, how do we adaptively sustain discipline when turmoil threatens to derail progress? The research-backed answers may surprise us.

Counterintuitively, studies on setbacks reveal that doubling down on preexisting positive habits breeds resilience rather than reactively quitting goals for temporary refuge (Rogers, 2023). Because adversity inherently disorients, clinging to disciplined pillars lends stability when other structures crumble. Our mindset strengthens, seeing we've overcome before.

Counterintuitively, studies on setbacks reveal that doubling down on preexisting positive habits breeds resilience rather than reactively quitting goals for temporary refuge (Rogers, 2023). Because adversity inherently disorients, clinging to disciplined pillars lends stability when other structures crumble. Our mindset strengthens, seeing we've overcome before.

Additionally, injecting mini-rewards between difficult sprints recharges depleted willpower stores that scarcity mindsets exhaust faster. Tiny wins refuel. Finally, getting tactically ruthless about protecting sleep, nutrition, and movement no matter the external chaos provides biological aid, powering perseverance internally.

When trying to reach a big goal, it can feel hopeless at times. In those moments, it helps to focus on positive habits and routines that are already working well rather than giving up entirely. Celebrate small wins along the way, like sticking to a study schedule or making progress bit by bit. Finding internal motivation through existing good habits and pacing yourself with achievable milestones is key.

The next time chaos strikes, remember: your self-discipline sweet spot lies nearby, awaiting activation through simple science-based adjustments conservatively steering energy toward the light.

Harnessing Technology for Self-Discipline

In an age of perpetual digital distraction threatening productivity, perhaps technology itself offers us pathways for combatting wavering willpower. By thoughtfully utilizing apps and web tools strategically blocking procrastination hooks, we install external motivational scaffolding precisely when internal reserves feel drained. Let's explore research-backed techniques leveraging tech assistance to automate consistent self-discipline where unplugged efforts falter over time.

Web blockers provide the most direct intervention, restricting access to chronically distracting sites like social media and newsfeeds that derail workflows. Tools like Freedom, Cold Turkey, and Website Blocker curate custom blacklists while locking options during designated work blocks so willpower doesn't waste energy batting away temptations. Set it and forget it productivity support.

Accountability apps similarly harness external pressure for consistency where solo attempts at habit formation unravel over weeks. Coach.me, Stickk, and HabitShare allow registering goals and then tracking adherence metrics viewable by peer groups. Public progress feels more motivational for software-based cheerleaders checking if we've fulfilled Fitbit steps, completed Duolingo lessons, or whatever micro-behaviors inch toward dreams.

Focus booster apps help laser attention, too, by gamifying concentration sprints and then rewarding mindful effort with break timers. Forest challenges users to stay off phones during work intervals lest cute, planted tree sprites digitally perish from neglect! Productivity timers like Tomato Aldo visualize ticking countdown clocks signaling the next opportunity for relief. Building delayed gratification tolerance strengthens self-discipline over time.

Away from screens, simple analog solutions enhance accountability, too. Handwritten journaling and visible progress charts significantly increase follow-through where digital life scatters direction. Bullet journals infusing artistic flair and checklist accomplishments retain multi-sensory impact, unlocking motivation. Vision boards displaying milestone rewards manifest urgency fueling discipline's last mile.

While inner work-building perseverance matters most in the long-term, don't underestimate supplemental digital tools accelerating success during vulnerable beginnings of habit formation. Try stacking the odds for consistency in your favor by letting artificial intelligence block sites subverting workflows. Broadcast public goal metrics celebrating micro-wins that accumulate major transformation. Divert online distractions to empower self-discipline shining through.

Executive Functioning Skills and Self-Discipline

Beyond raw willpower, the brain's executive functioning capacities deeply shape self-discipline outcomes, too. What are these pivotal cognitive skills, and how can we cultivate them to defeat procrastination?

Executive functions organize, prioritize, initiate, and sustain goal-driven behaviors. Think conductor coordinating the mental orchestra. Core components include attentional control, working memory, inhibitory control, cognitive flexibility, and more.

When executive functioning flows smoothly, we plan thoroughly and then follow through, resisting distraction. We start tasks avoiding paralysis despite discomfort. We persist through roadblocks, adapting strategies flexibly without abandoning aims. Future consequences feel tangible, informing wise choices. In other words, self-discipline shines!

However, executive dysfunction scrambles these critical processes. We epitomize "all gas, no brakes," lacking impulse control while juggling competing demands. Tasks overwhelm working memory, so we quit prematurely. Tunnel vision rigidly clings to plans despite irrelevance.

Disorganization breeds chaos without structure. Hello, procrastination!

While some executive functioning challenges originate biologically, purposeful training expands capacities significantly. So, how do you upgrade?

Start by identifying unique deficits, then target training. Those struggling with distraction benefit from optimizing focus stamina through mindfulness, meditation, and removing digital temptations. If inadequate planning derails follow-through, build systems. Feel paralyzed kicking off goals? Draft implementation intention scripts for when/then behavioral cues. Just know your personal weakness, and then strategically strengthen it.

Establish consistency, too. Like physical exercise, mental skills need regular training before fluently accessing them during crunch times. Schedule short daily sessions for your workbook tasks, 15 minutes practicing focused attention or planning projects, and sticking to timelines without abandoning them halfway. Journal accomplishments helping track growth.

Infuse novelty, stimulating working memory and inhibitory control, too. Learn new skills, travel unfamiliar routes, and alternate household chores. Pursue creative hobbies and complex games. Seek weird ideas and diverse perspectives, expanding thinking. The brain thrives on cognitive complexity!

Finally, embed desired actions into existing habit cues through conditioning to bypass dependence on conscious effort alone. Over time, executive functioning flows automatically without sole reliance on depletion-prone self-control. Slowly, improved functioning reduces procrastination vulnerability through aligned systems supporting progress!

Case Studies: Self-Discipline in Action

We've now extensively explored research foundations behind manifesting consistent self-discipline by progressing from psychological underpinnings to tangible habit-stacking routines and more. But how do these insights translate into reality-tested outcomes when applied by actual people seeking motivation transformation? Let's bring the science to life through uplifting case studies!

Meet Serena, an aspiring fiction writer who always seemed to put off dedicated creative time thanks to an energy-zapping corporate job. However, when a doctor mandated moving daily for health, suddenly making space for morning writing sprints before work got effortlessly integrated by piggybacking atop the non-negotiable new walking routine. Tiny acts accreted into mighty momentum even amid 60-hour workweeks!

Or examine Noah, a talented youth soccer coach who struggled to maintain his workout regimen during seasons when practices spiked. Rather than quitting temporarily as usual, Noah committed simply to doing two minutes of bodyweight exercises in his kitchen before brushing his teeth each night as an arbitrary baseline through chaos. Surprisingly, these micro-habits glued into comeback conditioning, allowing a graceful return to full training afterward.

In both cases, the key to sustaining self-discipline through exhaustion or adversity lay in sticking with seemingly "too small" positive rituals layered into existing regimens before strain arose. But tiny grains accumulated into transformation mountains as identity shifted toward resilience. Where friction once immobilized, disciplined living shines possible through science-guided configuration!

Exercise: Self Reflect

Now that we've extensively toured the foundations behind building lasting self-discipline, the next step becomes internalizing insights through application. Knowledge remains theoretical until tested and refined incrementally in our unique contexts.

Reflection Questions:

What self-discipline thought patterns or behaviors do you frequently struggle with that sabotage progress (all-or-nothing thinking, distraction addiction, etc.)? Dig deeper into the root causes.

Review suggested research-backed strategies covered, choosing two to three small, realistic tactics for testing counter-measures given your insights.

Troubleshoot micro habit experiments by applying those tactics for two weeks. Chart any correlations. What tangible gains accumulated? What still needs refinement?

Journaling Exercise:

Make a T-chart. On the left, write a stalled goal where self-discipline has crumbled. On the right, journal how building mini habits could create positive momentum.

Affirmation:

"Through small steps today, my self-discipline compounds breakthroughs."

Action Step:

Commit to one tiny habit aligned with a wavering goal. Just get momentum!

I hope that through tailored experimentation, you'll increasingly transform self-sabotaging patterns into self-directed progress through compounding micro-wins.

Applying Self-Discipline Insights

We've covered extensive ground exploring the psychology and tactics manifesting self-discipline—from intrinsic motivation sparks and deliberate habit stacking to resistance resilience features and time management tricks, plus the power of crafted cues and reframing mindset narratives toward possibility. Such knowledge is useless without action, so where do you begin uniquely applying it all in your life?

First, start identifying any dysfunctional assumptions potentially sabotaging subconscious beliefs around your self-discipline capacities. Do you perceive willpower as strictly limited? Confuse goal flexibility with a lack of direction? View setbacks as definitive evidence of impossibility? Surface then reframe stories blocking progress.

Next, script a few micro-habits supporting overarching aims, seeking outlets piggybacking existing routine cures. What quick actions, repeated daily, create compounding momentum? How can we engineer conditions that make small gains unavoidable? Follow the discipline's path of least resistance.

Finally, preemptively install organizational buffers and boundary guardrails protecting recurring rhythms from disruption when crises strike—plan recovery protocols not as reflective breakdown responses but as proactive resilience cultivation when we feel strongest.

Through these basic building blocks alone, assumption investigation, micro-habit stacking, and adversity-proofing measures, we massively upgrade self-discipline skills with time as tiny gains multiply, delivering compound strengths.

Wrapping Up...

In closing, we've covered immense ground exploring the science of manifesting self-discipline, from psychological foundations to tangible habit stacking structures to cultivating grit and more. The key realization? With knowledge plus application, we each hold the power to transform lifelong delay tendencies and instead forge motivate paths aligned to core values through incremental progress.

What once seemed impossible shines brightly viable when we wisely support human behavior's mysterious machinery instead of straining against it. Tiny gains truly do compound into massive mountains when consistently pursued.

Of course, the journey requires courage, compassion for ourselves and others when inevitable backslides hit, and recurring efforts to tweak systems until they fit our unique needs. There will always be turbulence on the open waters. But with charts directing to True North purpose etched deeply onto our vessel hulls through practices explored here, arrival in time grows assured if we but persist through the winds one stroke in front of the last.

Chapter 7: Mindfulness and Focus

With the number of websites, videos, podcasts, work tasks, and more all competing for your attention, focus can be hard to find, and that's exactly why it's so vital. When distractions nip at us from all sides, keeping our minds anchored takes some serious mental muscle.

That brings us to mindfulness. Mindfulness means directing your attention to the present, gently noticing thoughts without getting tangled up in them. Easier said than done, I know. However, research confirms that mindfulness actually strengthens your brain's focusing skills (Budson, 2021).

How does being unfocused fuel procrastination? More than you'd think. Each distraction pulls you that much further from tough tasks. Over time, you start avoiding work altogether since it now feels downright unpleasant. Scrolling social media for the 327th time suddenly seems way nicer. See the problem? Mindfulness breaks this vicious cycle, helping you dial down distractions and reel that wandering mind back into the now.

This chapter will guide you through research-backed mindfulness techniques for locking in laser focus. We'll cover the basics of mindfulness and then tackle real-world applications, from mindful communication to defusing distracting coworkers. With vivid examples along the way, you'll gather ideas for sprinkling mindfulness into your day. My aim is to equip you with concrete tools for sharpening your attention and dissolving procrastination triggers. Get ready to boost your mental stamina.

Foundations of Mindfulness

Before we dive into specific applications, let's build a solid base understanding of what mindfulness actually entails. At its core, mindfulness means maintaining present-moment awareness with openness and curiosity. Rather than getting tangled up in regrets, worries, or distractions, mindful awareness anchors you in the now.

Mindfulness asks us to pay attention to thoughts and physical sensations, observing them nonjudgmentally as they arise and pass away. When frustration, boredom, or excitement show up, notice how these feelings manifest in the body and mind without reacting or following where they lead. The key is cultivating self-awareness and acceptance.

In practical terms, mindfulness gets strengthened through formal meditation and informal practice. Meditation involves reserving blocks of time to tune into breath and bodily sensations. But we also cultivate mindfulness by bringing nonjudgmental attention to everyday activities, washing dishes, walking the dog, and having conversations.

Mindfulness Meditation Benefits

Mindfulness meditation serves as the primary formal method for building present-moment awareness. Although practices vary, most center on sitting comfortably and focusing attention on the physical sensations of each inhale and exhale. When the mind inevitably wanders, gently return focus to the breath without self-criticism. Start with 5-10 minutes daily, allowing the practice to reveal the workings of your mind.

Research shows meditation boosts attentional control, reduces mind wandering, and activates brain regions related to focus (Budson, 2021). Among procrastinators, it decreases avoiding behaviors, anxiety, and perfectionism. Beyond strengthening concentration, mindfulness meditation also lowers stress, increases creativity, and enhances overall well-being. These are added perks in overcoming chronic delay!

Cultivating Present-Moment Awareness

Beyond formal meditation, we can cultivate mindfulness throughout daily life. Try incorporating present-moment awareness into routine activities. While washing dishes or brushing your teeth, tune into the physical sensations—the warmth of the water and the feel of the sponge or brush. When walking, consciously note each foot touching the ground. During conversations, listen attentively to the speaker's words without planning your response.

Set reminders to pause throughout the day, taking a few mindful breaths. Observe passing thoughts and emotions without reacting. Strategically place items around your home or office to remind you to come back to the present: a sparkling crystal, a vibrant image, or even your watch.

It also helps to conduct mundane tasks differently to spark mindfulness. Brush your teeth with the hand you don't usually use. Walk your usual route backward. Take varied routes between home and work. Shake up habits to reveal the novelty all around you.

Approach daily encounters with heightened curiosity and playfulness, too. Fully engage your senses in routine dinner prep, the pungent garlic, crisp sound of chopping veggies. Notice wildlife on neighborhood walks. Appreciate the rich array of colors and textures filling your world.

The key is gently encouraging mindful moments without forcing them. With consistent practice, present-moment attention grows into a habit, organically expanding your capacity for focus. By infusing mindfulness throughout life's nooks and crannies, you equip yourself to meet procrastination triggers with less resistance.

Mindfulness and Focus in Work

Just as mindfulness strengthens focus in daily living, bringing present-moment awareness to the workplace unlocks productivity. When facing a laborious report or endless inbox, remember to anchor yourself in the here and now before diving in.

Scan the body for areas of tightness or tension. Soften these spots as you tune into the physical sensations of breathing. Observe passing thoughts without following tangents. Appreciate elements like the feel of the keyboard under your fingertips or sunlight streaming through the window—this simple act of checking in grounds you in the present, dialing down distractions.

From this mindful state, plunge into your tasks with undivided attention. When you catch the mind wandering, gently return focus to the work at hand. I know, easier said than done. Start small by bringing mindful attention to individual emails or meetings.

Set random reminders to pause throughout the day, directing attention inward for a few moments before redirecting it outward. Keep centering anchors nearby - affirmation cards, vision boards, and meaningful trinkets. Sit upright while working to boost engagement.

Schedule mindfulness breaks, too, for 5-10 minutes in the middle of large projects. During these pauses, tune into your senses, stretch consciously, and grab a nourishing snack. Don't check devices! Use breaks to truly rest attention. With consistent practice, integrating mindfulness into workflow strengthens concentration, boosts energy, and reduces procrastination's tempting pull.

Overcoming Distractions Through Mindfulness

Let's face it: with texts and Slack pings, nearby coworkers, and inner worries, staying focused amid distractions often feels downright impossible. This is where mindfulness saves the day. By continually returning wandering attention to the present, we build incredible mental stamina.

Practice acknowledging distractions without following or reacting to them. Feel that familiar itch to check your phone? Note "urge to check phone," maybe label it as anticipation, anxiety, or boredom without judgment. Scan emotions that arise just like clouds passing through the sky. Return focus to the task at hand.

Or getting distracted by a loud coworker conversation? Carefully note what drew your attention, then redirect awareness to physical sensations that anchor you, perhaps breath or hands touching the keyboard. Come back to the present with patience and compassion.

Incorporate mindfulness practices first thing in the morning or when struggling to concentrate. Meditate for a few minutes, establishing a calm, clear mental space conducive to undistracted work. You train the brain to grow those precious focus muscles.

It also helps to streamline and organize tasks ahead of time. Declutter digital spaces, create efficient systems for managing information and strategically block distraction-prone websites. Combining these concrete steps with mindfulness builds essential internal and external conditions for defeating persistent diversions. Stay committed, and distractions become less magnetic over time as you strengthen your focus.

Mindfulness-Based Stress Reduction

As an unavoidable workplace reality, stress often fuels procrastination tendencies. Mindfulness offers a potent antidote. By cultivating present-focused awareness, we dial down anxiety and perfectionism, circumventing delay.

Mindfulness-based stress reduction (MBSR) centers on accepting rather than struggling with uncomfortable thoughts and emotions. Physical sensations offer portals for tuning into stress. Tense muscles, shallow breathing, and fatigue all provide entry points for investigation.

Start by taking a few minutes during stressful periods to investigate bodily sensations. Where does tension accumulate? Jaw? Shoulders? Stomach? Soften and breathe into these areas while labeling emotions with curiosity, not judgment. This helps short-circuit the anxiety loop, preventing a downward procrastination spiral.

Come back to sensory anchors that ground you in the present moment, a warm cup of tea, photos of loved ones, and five things you can see. Deliberately shift focus toward these sensations without following stressful thoughts down the rabbit hole.

Strengthen coping skills further through mindfulness meditation, consciously transforming the relationship between discomfort and work. Difficult emotions like boredom, anxiety, and frustration will undoubtedly arise during challenging projects. Note these feelings, investigate associated physical sensations, then refocus attention on the breath.

Repeat this process patiently over time. As mindfulness grows, you relate to discomfort differently, with less avoidance. Stress holds less power in derailing progress. You tackle tedious tasks with steadiness, empowered through mindful presence to override procrastination's strong pull.

Mindful Decision-Making

Procrastination often stems from impulsive decisions rooted in momentary cravings rather than intentional choice. Mindfulness counters this tendency by cultivating self-awareness and deliberate focus when facing decisions. By tuning into our mental and emotional landscape, we choose responses consciously rather than reactively.

The first step is noticing when important choices arise. Perhaps you must decide whether to accept an exciting but demanding project or delegate a subset of recurring tasks. When these decisive moments pop up, pause rather than default to habit.

Tune into physical sensations, emotions, and thoughts swirling internally. Label feelings and assumptions without judgment. Then, broaden attention outward to consider contextual factors shaping the decision, priorities, values, and long-term goals.

From this grounded state, identify potential paths forward, weighing the pros and cons of each with clarity. Recognize both logic and intuition. Ultimately, make choices aligned with deeper priorities rather than fleeting impulses.

Weave mindfulness practices into daily rituals, too, for routines like when to start and end work. Bookend your workday with 10 mindful breaths. At the start, set intentions; what meaningful priorities will drive decisions today? Before leaving, reflect on how choices aligned with these aims. Make deliberate tweaks day to day rather than operating on autopilot.

With consistent training, mindfulness creates cushions between impulse and action. We respond thoughtfully vs. automatically, escaping traps that feed procrastination. Aligned decisions become second nature.

Mindful Communication

Beyond personal focus and decision-making, mindfulness also unlocks connection and understanding between people, capacities absolutely essential for reducing procrastination. By cultivating present-focused attention, we communicate with greater empathy, honesty, and clarity.

Start by bringing mindful awareness to conversations and meetings, whether with bosses, colleagues, or clients. Before jumping to form a response while others speak, consciously focus on the words being exchanged without judgment. What core emotions and perspectives emerge?

Approach each interaction as wholly unique rather than relying on familiar roles or power dynamics. Set aside assumptions as best possible to receive each individual clearly. Eliminate intrusive thoughts by gently returning attention to the speaker, the sound and cadence of their voice, and the use of eye contact and gestures.

Listen patiently until the person finishes conveying their main thoughts before asking clarifying questions or sharing your own perspective. Allow natural pauses between responses so you and others can integrate information thoughtfully.

When contributing your viewpoint, speak honestly but with compassion. Notice how your body feels: tension signals resistance, or ease indicates receptivity. Finding the calm mental space for truthful, caring dialogue prevents avoidance that feeds procrastination on collaborative projects.

Case Studies: Exemplifying Mindful Living

To ground mindfulness techniques in reality, let's explore how these skills transform procrastination tendencies in practice. Meet Sarah, Raj, and Nina, three professionals navigating distraction and delay to varying degrees. Through tailored mindfulness strategies, they each strengthen attention and unlock greater productivity.

Sarah constantly gets derailed from writing marketing materials by drifting into social media and surfing the news. To curb distractions, she designates daily 75-minute time blocks for focused project work. Before each block, Sarah meditates for 5 minutes, allowing mental clutter to settle before diving into writing. When Internet tangents grab her attention, she pauses and breathes consciously, redirecting awareness to the words before her eyes until absorption returns.

For Raj, an accountant, restlessness and boredom while poring over financial documents often lead to snacking or drawn-out water cooler conversations. He sets a bell nearby, reminding him to take quick, mindful breaks every 45 minutes. During these pauses, Raj tunes into bodily sensations scans his visual landscape appreciatively and takes a few deep breaths. This disruptive stimulus helps Raj return to spreadsheets feeling refreshed and focused.

As a nurse practitioner, Nina's active medical work makes traditional seated meditation challenging. Instead, she cultivates informal mindfulness practices between patients, mindfully sanitizing hands, focusing fully on one chart at a time, and chewing food deliberately during short breaks. Feeling emotionally or mentally depleted, Nina finds quiet spaces to tune into breathing, softening tension through conscious exhalations. This attunement breaks distraction patterns, energizing her for the next patient encounters.

As these stories illustrate, creative applications of mindfulness can transform limiting patterns, empowering deepened attention and engagement in all facets of work. The more individuals who fine-tune these skills, the further procrastination tendencies recede from view.

Overcoming Barriers to Mindfulness

Like any skill worth cultivating, mindfulness asks for patience and persistence. Despite good intentions, you'll inevitably face obstacles interfering with regular practice. Typical hurdles include lack of time, fatigue, misperceptions, difficulty sitting still, and impatience with the gradual process. Understand these stumbling blocks as natural rather than signs you can't build mindfulness. Arm yourself with the following strategies for sticking with and even coming to enjoy stillness practices.

If you feel too busy for meditation, remember just 5-10 minutes of mindful breathing builds focus over time. Even one minute makes a difference! Schedule mindfulness into each day like other priorities. Set reminders on your calendar or ask supportive friends and family to help reinforce the habit. Discover odd moments for practice, waiting in line, before meetings, and waking up.

Fatigue and restlessness also commonly block consistency. Counter this by practicing mindfulness in motion, like mindful walking or household chores. Do body scans while lying in bed. Splash cold water on your face beforehand or stretch consciously to rouse energy. Deepen focus through intriguing objects like candle flames or captivating nature photos. Experiment to find what clicks.

You may grapple with misperceptions, too, such as that mindfulness requires clearing all thoughts or sitting perfectly still. Remember, the practice involves gently returning attention to anchor points like the breath when it wanders, allowing whatever arises without frustration. Maintain reasonable goals like five mindful minutes or simply notice when your mind leaves the present. Build positive associations with mindfulness through consistency and self-care.

Sitting meditation also proves challenging for those who struggle with stillness. No problem! Try mindful walking, yoga, riding the bus, washing dishes—any activity lending itself to present focus. For those unable to close their eyes, incorporate visual cues like candles, inspiring images, or nature views. Over time, your capacity for seated practice likely expands as focus gets trained.

Above all, summon patience. As a fundamental life skill, mindfulness unfolds in fits and starts. Some days, concentration soars, and other times, boredom or distraction seem impossible to transcend. Expect ups and downs, and meet yourself where you're at with compassion. Trust that the more consistently you nurture mindful attention, however imperfectly, the more this capacity takes root.

Mindfulness for Decision Fatigue

By day's end, making even small choices feels agonizing. You stand paralyzed before the overflowing fridge, blankly reread the same email, unable to respond, and deliberate for ages what podcast to play during your commute. Sound familiar? Welcome to decision fatigue. After hours of problem-solving and directing attention at work, our willpower gets tapped out just when personal priorities call for conscious choice. Cue avoidance behaviors that feed procrastination. This is where mindfulness saves the day. By anchoring our wavering mental energies in the present, mindfulness regenerates cognitive bandwidth depleted by demanding focus throughout work hours. We end days empowered by inner clarity rather than paralyzed by overwhelm when facing decisions.

Start cultivating mindfulness as early in your workday as possible. Before diving into demanding cognitive tasks, establish focus through 5-10 minutes of anchoring awareness on the breath and bodily sensations. This centers the brain's spotlight on perceptions flowing through the present rather than ruminating on past or future concerns that drain energy over time.

Use mindfulness to regularly disrupt rumination and distraction loops mid-day, too. Set a timer for every 60-90 minutes, prompting you to tune into somatic cues for a few minutes. Soften tension with deep breaths while pivoting attention from screens and outer stimuli inward. By consciously connecting with your inner landscape, you short-circuit draining thoughts from escalating into decision anxiety later on. Stay ahead of creeping mental fatigue.

Strategically integrate mindfulness into transitional moments between intense concentration as well. After completing complex analytical reports or customer calls requiring razor-sharp presence, pause before immediately jumping into another elongated knowledge work session. First, mindfully scan bodily sensations, soften tension spots, and follow the breath for a few minutes to let one mental muscle rest before straining the next set. Layer in these purposeful attention pivots to regularly replenish cognitive resources that decision-making draws on.

Double down on mindfulness resets when work concludes before commuting or transitioning to personal responsibilities. Rather than letting work thoughts bleed into evening hours, establish strong mental brackets bookending your effort. Pause to meditate or at least take a few minutes tuning into the senses that immerse you into off-the-clock consciousness. Mindfully preparing dinner, hugging loved ones, or walking the dog shifts gears into modes where decision energy can be restored overnight. Protect precious recovery time rather than exhausting it by ruminating over the workday.

By cementing mindfulness into your daily flow, you reinforce the muscle memory needed to keep present-focused attention ever accessible. Whenever willpower for optimal choices wanes, instantly tap this grounding skillset.

Meet critical intersections with clear eyes undistorted by depletion. Mindfulness makes each small choice conscious again rather than taxed. And collectively, aligned decision-making fuels substantial positive change once procrastination's interference gets neutralized. Start reclaiming your precious inner resources one mindful minute at a time!

Exercise: Self Reflect

The key to unlocking mindfulness practices is consistent experimentation tailored to your life. Let these questions guide you.

Reflection Questions:

What types of tasks or situations especially diminish your focus and concentration? Meetings? Tedious work? Identify the trouble spots.

When distracted or avoiding important work, what repeated thoughts arise? Self-doubt? Perfectionism? Boredom? Name the key triggers.

Journaling Exercise:

Make a T-chart. On the left, jot down activities prone to mind wandering. On the right, brainstorm ideas for infusing mindful attention.

Affirmation:

"I gently return my attention to the present moment."

Action Step:

Pick one distracted task this week. Infuse five minutes of mindful attention before diving in. Just build focus muscles!

We hope these reflections and experiments help strengthen your mindfulness muscle, allowing increased focus towards priorities that enhance productivity and fulfillment. Keep nurturing attention with compassion!

Practical Outcomes: Infusing

Mindfulness Into Daily Life

As we've discovered, cultivating mindfulness and razor-sharp focus serves as a pivotal key to overcoming procrastination. By continually reining in attention to the present, we relate to tasks—however mundane or difficult, with less judgment and avoidance. Progress becomes fueled by clarity rather than compromised by distraction.

We've covered a spectrum of techniques for strengthening mindful presence, ranging from meditation and strategic reminders to sensory awareness practices. Tailor these tools to your own work style and personality. Experiment with reminders like apps, post-its, timers, or use objects with sensory impact. Identify optimal times for formal mindfulness practice.

Infuse mindfulness into activities you find boring or stressful. How about mindful data entry, where you tune into the sensations of typing? Or washing dishes more consciously, noticing soap bubbles and sounds? Discover creative bridges between mindfulness and obligations that tempt procrastination.

Make mindfulness a lifestyle, not just another task. Let present-focused attention permeate your work and relationships. Listen to loved ones attentively without planning responses. Savor morning coffee or the walk home with heightened awareness. Establish queues for redirecting attention inward throughout the day.

Stay patient with occasional mind wandering; simply return to the now with self-compassion. Over time, mindfulness becomes second nature, providing a grounded place from which to meet daily responsibilities and challenges proactively. You step into your potential, propelled by clarity rather than hemmed in by disruptive diversions.

Wrapping Up...

As we bring our exploration of mindfulness and focus to a close, I hope you feel empowered by the incredible potential of present-moment awareness. We've covered everything from the research-backed benefits of mindfulness to practical workplace applications, managing distractions, communicating mindfully, and even boosting decision-making.

Most importantly, you now have a versatile toolkit for overcoming procrastination by continually reining in wandering attention. Tailor these techniques to your own tendencies and tasks. Infuse mindfulness into activities you find boring or stressful. Discover creative bridges between mindful presence and project obligations that tempt delay.

Make mindfulness a lifestyle, not just another item on your to-do list. Let this grounded, nonjudgmental awareness permeate your work and relationships. Listen without planning responses, savor ordinary moments more fully, and establish cues to redirect attention inward. The more mindfulness sinks into life's fabric, the less likely distractions snag you.

Trust that occasional mind wandering is perfectly normal; simply return to the now with patience and self-compassion. Over time, present-focused clarity becomes your steady basecamp for proactive progress. You step fully into each responsibility and priority, free from procrastination's paralyzing grip.

As the case studies illustrated, creative applications of mindfulness can rewire even lifelong distraction patterns. So stay committed through ups and downs, infusing mindful engagement into your days. With consistent nurturing of this mental muscle, you'll breeze through tasks that once fueled avoidance.

Chapter 8:
Handling Setbacks

Setbacks are those unexpected curveballs on your journey that push your productivity plans off course, falling into procrastination pitfalls, missing deadlines that seemed in reach, and encountering obstacles that stall progress.

Not what your momentum-craving, success-starved brain wants to hear. But resisting life's stumbles only brings more suffering. These apparent detours along our growth path are guaranteed if you're genuinely pushing limits. And while setbacks indeed complicate the ride, they also unlock our greatest potential if handled with care.

Instead of resigning yourself to misery when challenges arise, get curious! How can this challenge nourish your perseverance? Build compassion? Reveal blind spots that, once cleaned up, will make you wiser and more attuned to what truly matters.

My aim is to provide that nourishing mindset, combined with research-backed strategies, allowing you to squeeze growth opportunities from every setback. You'll learn to objectively assess what knocked you off track, adapt goals accordingly, and rebuild momentum stronger than before.

I hope you walk away viewing hurdles along the path as step-up opportunities rather than step-outs forcing you to quit. Stumbles show you're daring greatly. And daring greatly is the only way to achieve greatness.

Understanding the Nature of Setbacks

To strategically bounce back from setbacks, let's first break down what derailments tend to arise around procrastination specifically. Common backward slides include:

- **Losing motivation:** After a focused period, feeling that initial drive to change habits taper off. Difficulty sustaining effort over time.

- **Goal abandonment:** Completely abandoning an objective you set out to accomplish without consciously reassessing.

- **Time mismanagement:** Reverting to poor time management habits that allow tasks to pile up.

- **Distraction relapse:** Getting continually pulled by digital diversions/other temptations that sabotage productivity.

- **Perfection paralysis:** Falling back into extreme perfectionistic tendencies that inhibit getting work done.

- **Task avoidance:** Hitting periods when even starting projects feels overwhelmingly unpleasant, heightening procrastination.

Take note of which of these pitfalls particularly plague you so we can tailor effective turnaround strategies.

Beyond external consequences, setbacks also deliver a hefty psychological blow. Our ego takes a hit, diminishing self-confidence in achieving goals after repeated failures or mistakes. Feelings of frustration, shame, anxiety, and overwhelm frequently arise too.

Brimming optimism gives way to disempowering thoughts: "I just can't seem to change my chronic procrastination. I'll always fall short when it matters most." Sound familiar? This mental narrative then fuels further retreat into what's comfortable, distraction, and delay. Vicious cycle alert!

But difficult emotions are not something to battle or "fix." Approach them with curiosity, patience, and care. Allow any turbulence stirred up by setbacks to settle rather than suppressing it forcefully. Once you establish steadiness of mind, you gain the necessary perspective for moving ahead constructively after pitfalls rather than spiraling.

Resilience as a Procrastination Antidote

If setbacks inevitably arise, how do we keep inching forward? Resilience! This pivotal capacity to recover after adversities, missteps, and challenges prevents procrastination from permanently derailing progress.

Resilience refunds our belief in ourselves even when temporarily shaken, allowing us to bounce back wiser and more committed to positive change. It gives us faith to try again in the face of repeated failures. Developing resilience transforms obstacles from breaking points into breakthroughs.

Thankfully, resilience originates from skills we can nurture rather than fixed personality traits. Key techniques include:

- **Reframing perspective:** Viewing setbacks as inherent to achievement rather than personal flaws or poor luck. Even Olympic athletes and esteemed scientists experience countless stumbles!

- **Support systems:** Surrounding yourself with those who reassure your inherent strengths and capacity for high achievement despite temporary setbacks. Social support protects against discouragement.

- **Self-care:** Prioritize healthy lifestyle factors like sufficient sleep, balanced nutrition and regular movement to manage stress and maintain emotional equilibrium through ups and downs.

- **Learning from errors:** Analyzing each setback objectively rather than ignoring or ruminating on missteps. Extract lessons, then let go with self-compassion.

The more we utilize such strategies through minor and major tribulations, the more our resilience muscle naturally grows. What once felt devastating we eventually take in stride as fuel for continued effort.

Analyzing Setbacks: Lessons Learned

When you hit those inevitable setbacks on your path to enhanced productivity, avoid getting swallowed by discouragement. Reframe the situation as an opportunity for growth by deeply analyzing what went awry.

Resist pointing fingers at situational factors or your own inadequacy as the culprit. Setbacks rarely stem from a single cause. Instead, reflect on the full range of potential influences with openness to gain practical wisdom for moving ahead, including:

- **Environmental triggers:** Distracting work ambiance? Competing home demands? Poor work-life balance?

- **Knowledge/skill gaps:** Do you need more expertise in certain time management techniques or communication strategies to achieve set goals?

- **Overly ambitious timelines:** We're often overly optimistic about how quickly new habits form. Reassess reasonable rates of progression.

Extracting even one beneficial insight makes the setback worthwhile, allowing improved strategies so future efforts align better with reality.

Just as important as pinpointing external causes is fostering a constructive mindset when your momentum stalls out. As tough as it feels when projects derail, or motivation dwindles, mentally clinging to the bigger picture, you're progressing along a winding path to overcome deep-rooted procrastination patterns. That brings inevitable ups and downs.

Recall times when you navigated major tribulations that caused doubts about other meaningful quests ongoing in your life. How can those resilient mindsets apply now? Ground yourself in the core aspirations that make this effort worthwhile, be it reduced anxiety, greater professional credibility, or freedom from procrastination's burden in your most precious domains.

From this wise vantage point, you view setbacks as inherent to any growth process rather than personal defects or poor luck. They inform your strategy and strengthen your courage. Though the emotional sting naturally remains, your sense of discouragement soon transforms into an informed, compassionate commitment.

Strategies for Effective Setback Management

Once you've extracted all possible lessons from a given procrastination setback, shift focus to pragmatic revival strategies so you can get back on track swiftly and wisely. Useful research-backed tactics include:

- **Reviewing progress made rather than just lost:** Validate any positive strides forward before reviewing the setback, even if they now feel eclipsed. Hold onto evidence that you can achieve the desired changes.

- **Updating routines and environmental cues:** Refresh daily schedules, to-do lists, workspace setup, and reminder systems to spark renewed motivation after it wanes.

- **Rewarding small steps:** For tasks that now trigger avoidance due to a setback, establish mini-milestones with built-in rewards to regain positive associations.

- **Adding accountability:** Communicate openly about the setback with supportive contacts who can cheer the constructive steps you take to resume progress.

- **Practicing self-compassion:** Rather than beating yourself up, talk to yourself internally with the kindness and reassurance you would offer a close friend in your shoes.

In tandem with such momentum-building tricks, thoughtfully readjust goals or timelines thrown off track by setbacks. Gather insight from the analytical process about which objectives need refinement given current abilities and constraints.

Redefine what satisfactory progress looks like for now based on learnings, perhaps completing 2 crucial portfolio pieces rather than 5. Or consistently working on projects for 45 minutes each weekday morning vs. 90 minutes daily. Unless changes directly conflict with core aspirations, remain flexible.

Review this updated roadmap regularly, continuing to edit signposts that guide you toward gradually enhanced productivity. With self-compassion infusing the entire process, you turn setbacks into step-up opportunities, quickening your transformation.

Coping with Emotional Responses to Setbacks

Beyond practical hurdles, setbacks also kick up a wave of challenging emotions—frustration, anxiety, shame, and overwhelm. The initial enthusiasm fueling your procrastination-busting efforts gets replaced by disempowering thoughts: "I just can't seem to change. What's the point in trying?"

Rather than resisting or ignoring these feeling states, start by identifying emotions that arise for you when projects derail, or motivation falters. Which crop up most fiercely, anger? Hopelessness? Resentment? Allow them space to fully play out.

Suppressing natural responses often backfires, leaking out later as self-sabotage. Safely contacting the depth of any churned-up feelings helps release their intensity so you regain the necessary perspective.

As emotional storms pass through following setbacks, employ research-backed coping strategies to settle any turbulence, including:

- Talking with trusted supports who simply listen without judgment as you unpack frustration or dismay.

- Journaling unfiltered emotional streams, then re-reading entries later with gentleness and objectivity.

- Voicing anger or grief through primal release practices like stomping, screaming, or sobbing into pillows.

- Letting imagery that captures your feelings flow freely onto paper through drawings and abstract paintings.

- Releasing tension through movement, long walks, punching bags, and dance.

By fully processing difficult emotions when productivity falters, you process rather than bypass them. This prevents destructive downstream impacts like giving up altogether or self-sabotage. You reignite motivation from a centered place.

Setback Recovery and Rebuilding

When challenging emotions stirred up by setbacks settle through processing and release, shift your energy toward steadfast rebuilding efforts. Double down on the practical momentum-regaining tactics we have covered so far, including refreshing routines, adding accountability channels, and celebrating small wins.

You may need to fully pull back and recalibrate in cases of major demolitions to your productivity infrastructure. But stay determined in the backswing return, one step at a time, one day at a time. Have faith that progress will steadily accumulate if rooted in self-compassion.

Beyond external behaviors, also actively nourish your inner terrain so motivation and focus flower again after wilting. Revisit your core aspirations, recalling the positive pull of what this overall procrastination reduction effort makes possible.

Immerse in activities that rouse your spirit and adventures in nature, listen to audio biographies of those you admire, and connect with supporters who remind you of your inherent greatness. Soon, creative energy bubbles up for pragmatic next steps.

To sustain regained traction after setback-induced slides, inject joyful mindfulness into your resurgent workflow. Appreciate subtle sensory pleasures, your toes touching the floor, and the vibrant sounds of birds outside your window. Notice the fulfillment of lost concentration returning.

Much like masterful athletes, they transmit laser-like, non-judgmental attention to tangible indicators of progress in tasks that further core goals. Keep perspective trained on the incremental gems of output emerging through steady applied effort rather than fixating on the endpoint.

Maintain physical and mental resilience by carving out frequent well-being boosting breaks for healthy snacks, revitalizing movement, or affirming personal check-ins amid reinstated diligence. By infusing intrinsic rewards into steps forward, motivation perpetuates.

Bouncing Back From Burnout

Repeated setbacks can drain our energy reserves, pushing us to the point of burnout, where we feel emotionally exhausted and struggle to make progress. Burnout often stems from unrelenting demands and not taking time to refuel properly. We deplete limited willpower trying to force output through sheer effort alone. Sound familiar?

When hitting this heavy phase, realize you've likely stretched personal bandwidth to its outer limits for too long without balancing renewal practices. Expect depleted motivation, fuzzy thinking, irritability, and fatigue. The solution lies not in pushing harder but rather in consciously recalibrating work-rest rhythms and strengthening mind-body resilience.

Start by taking a complete break from productivity efforts, even if just a few days, to reconnect with activities that rejuvenate depleted spirit, time in nature, social connection, and sensory pleasures like massage. Allow your nervous system to downshift out of fight-or-flight overload mode so you can access deeper wisdom for the next steps from a settled place.

As you transition back into workflow, carefully monitor energy levels so you don't overtax fragile reserves too quickly. Schedule mandatory renewal breaks every 60-90 minutes—walking outside and listening to uplifting music. Work in fragments with a power nap or snack breaks until concentration steadies. Celebrate micro-tasks accomplished through renewed engagement.

For the longer term, build emotional resilience to prevent future burnout slides through lifestyle pillars like sufficient sleep, balanced nutrition, and movement. Carve out periods for reflective replenishment, journaling, meditation, and creativity. Say no to added obligations that destabilize reasonable workloads. Release perfectionist tendencies for sustainable output that nourishes rather than drains.

When evaluating bigger picture changes after burnout, examine primary triggers that depleted inner resources. Is there a misalignment between responsibilities and authentic aspirations? Are workplace dynamics toxic or unstable? Do you lack connection to the deeper purpose of daily tasks? Leverage insights to guide any major restructuring so you rebuild workflow framed by meaning and self-knowledge.

By lovingly listening when over-tolerance of stress exhausts your precious internal resources, you summon the courage to honor limitations and pull back. Faith emerges that by profoundly realigning efforts with sustainable self-care practices, motivation naturally rebounds. Each burnout bout makes us wiser in balancing push with inner and outer nourishment.

Cultivating Courage Through Setbacks

Setbacks often reveal where fears and doubts hide in the shadowy corners of our psyche, only coming out when things get challenging. We may default to playing small rather than daring greatly when anxiety arises. But real courage means moving toward growth opportunities even when they trigger discomfort and uncertainty. How can we build the heroic mindset needed to convert setbacks into springboards?

Start by identifying limiting beliefs triggered when you encounter obstacles - perfectionism, self-doubt, comparison, imposter syndrome. Which inner voice warns, "You're not capable of achieving this goal" or "You'll never overcome chronic barriers"? Locate and challenge stories draining efforts of hope.

Gather empowering evidence disputing disempowering narratives. Recall previous challenges you navigated successfully despite difficulty academically, professionally, and relationally. Note strengths and values that fuel persistence. This builds self-trust to counter the next doomsday thought distortion, inflating the severity of the setback.

Expand your window of resilience so everyday hurdles seem surmountable, not catastrophic. Place past or present adversities on a spectrum from minor annoyance to severe crisis. Consider hardship experienced by historical or contemporary change-makers. Cultivate gratitude for current blessings. Stumbles gain perspective.

Surround yourself with a supportive community that embodies desired mindsets, conditioned optimism, and brave vulnerability. Their embodied wisdom and faith in your inherent abilities drown out inner hecklers. Feel courage transfer through compassionate allies who expect greatness despite occasional messiness.

Inject uplifting rituals into your workflow, celebrating small daily accomplishments, mindfulness of progress made, personal affirmations of capability and worthiness overlaid on tasks. Infuse spirit-nourishing movement and creativity breaks amid diligent sprints. Protecting intrinsic joy preserves motivation when obstacles arise.

By proactively growing the mental muscles needed to view setbacks as inherent to achievement, we gather the courage to respond with unstoppable conviction no matter how often we stumble. Our core confidence strengthens from repeatedly proving to ourselves that with disciplined effort and community support, we can persist through nearly any adversity, emerging stronger.

Case Studies: Transformative Setback Stories

Meet Max, Leila, and Richard, three individuals who faced challenging backslides when working to overcome chronic procrastination patterns getting in the way of their potential. Rather than let these reversals halt their positive momentum, they dug deep into their core aspirations and extracted lessons from the pitfalls, ultimately helping them create more fulfilling, productive lives.

Max, a digital marketer, hit a wall of distraction overload and complete work avoidance just months after significantly decreasing procrastination tendencies. In response, he consolidated to focus on one single revenue-driving campaign optimized with total presence. This targeted effort then created expansive confidence and clarity, allowing him to gradually integrate more responsibilities with undistracted engagement.

Leila, an abstract painter, became overwhelmed by paralyzing self-doubt after submitting work to a local gallery only to get rejected outright. However, leaning into ultra-supportive mentors helped strengthen her relationship with creative risk-taking. She gave herself permission to explore new styles without attachment to outcomes. Two years later, Leila's unique pieces were shown internationally.

As a software engineer, Richard got so despondent after dramatically missing a product deadline that he descended back into aimless scrolling. But once the initial anguish lessened, he initiated an open dialogue with colleagues about supporting each other through expected failures that are part of bold innovation. The cultural shift Richard sparked became the foundation for the team's greatest business breakthroughs.

As Max, Leila, and Richard's stories demonstrate, by proactively and courageously facing setbacks we inevitably encounter on all profound journeys, we unlock access to our highest level of purpose and contribution. Rather than defining us, setbacks refine us.

Exercise: Self Reflect

Setbacks sting at the moment but contain tremendous opportunity if excavated wisely. Let these prompts guide you.

Reflection Questions:

What recent setback derailed your productivity progress? How did the situation make you feel?

Analyze potential root causes honestly. What specifically threw you off track from goals or good habits?

Extract lessons: how can this experience inform your path ahead regarding realistic aims, necessary support, and blind spots to address?

Journaling Exercise:

Make a T-chart. On the left, jot down the setback situation. On the right, brainstorm constructive rebound steps, refreshed routines, accountability, celebrating small wins, etc.

Affirmation:

"I use stumbles as growth opportunities, becoming wiser and stronger."

Action Step:

Commit to one positive action restarting momentum after a recent setback. Gather lessons for the journey ahead!

By courageously assessing our stumbles and crafting constructive rebound plans, we reclaim agency over outcomes, abandoning the victim mentality. Setbacks transform into step-up opportunities, each one strengthening resilience so we show up powered-up for our highest purposes.

Practical Outcomes: Turning Setbacks Into Stepping Stones

By now, I hope you feel equipped with comprehensive techniques for wrestling, even soul-shaking stumbles into productive personal transformation. We covered objective setback analysis, adaptive goal-setting, coping through emotional trauma, extracting lessons, and ultimately resurging with redoubled efforts.

Remember, no matter how often you drift into counterproductive patterns, you can always tap resilience reserves and initiate accountability measures to guide you back to steady ground. Setback management skills grow each time we effectively apply them. Before long, we take what once felt utterly demolishing increasingly in stride, bolstered by an underlying sense of unstoppable forward momentum.

As you proceed positively through turbulent periods of regression, missteps, and revived attempts on your quest for long-term procrastination liberation, recall the transformation tales we explored. Like Max, Leila, and Richard, know that by courageously confronting each challenging twist and turn, you extract self-knowledge leading to your highest potential.

Use every apparent obstruction as a stepping stone toward increased personal power and purpose. When procrastination temporarily reemerges, remember to reinvigorate your core aspirations linked to enhanced productivity and life fulfillment. Maintain faith in your inner capacity to persist through muddy patches onto peaks, revealing wider vistas of what you can achieve.

Wrapping Up...

As we close this chapter on excavating diamonds from life's roughest terrains, I hope you feel equipped to alchemize setbacks into reinvigorated personal power. We covered everything from analyzing underlying causes, processing difficult emotions, adapting goals, and culminating with resilient rebuilding efforts.

Remember, no matter how frequently you slide into counterproductive ruts, you can always access untapped tenacity reserves by taking ownership of hurdles.

Setback management skills expand each time we effectively apply them. Before long, what once felt devastating gets embraced as a growth gift, strengthening effectiveness and self-trust.

As you proceed positively through turbulent times on your quest for enhanced productivity, recall the transformative tales we explored. Like Max, Leila, and Richard, know that by proactively mining obstructive situations for insight, you summon your highest potential while dismantling procrastination's drain.

Use every apparent obstruction as a stepping stone toward increased personal authority and purpose. Allow when delay tendencies flare up again to re-center your core aspirations linked to life fulfillment. Maintain faith in your inner capacity to persist through the mud onto peaks, revealing wider vistas of what you can achieve.

Conclusion

As we reach the final pages of our extensive exploration into the psychology of procrastination, I hope you feel empowered by the profound insights gained. We now understand this common struggle is not a reflection of laziness or poor time management but rather emotional regulation challenges combined with vicious anxiety cycles trapping our potential.

The following key realization brings peace: We can rewire engrained delay habits through motivation science strategies and self-awareness! Procrastination reflects learned patterns rather than innate flaws. By catching unproductive narratives early and taking small actions despite the discomfort, we walk liberated from perfectionistic paralysis. Our dreams glimmer progressively clearer until they are realized through courageous baby steps.

On this winding journey, we illuminated why short-term relief mechanisms feel tempting when goals intimidate us. We explored willpower gaps and biological cravings for instant dopamine versus earning delayed rewards through effort. Yet we also equipped ourselves with knowledge of the psychology technologies sparking inspiration despite such impulses.

Yes, setbacks will slow forward progress at times. But now, we have tangible resilience rituals for squeezing growth opportunities from every pitfall if we lean in with accountability and self-compassion. Each apparently demolished milestone becomes reconstructed stronger.

Clarity emerged too around lifestyle obstacles fueling procrastination when we disregard natural mental/physical rhythms needing balance. Through mindfulness, holistic nourishment, and boundary honoring, sustainability gets woven into ambition's fabric, so progress unfolds smoothly.

Of course, no formula fixes lifelong habits in a day. But the research-backed insights revealed here into emotional obstacles, chemical hooks, motivation, and mindfulness offer us immense power in consciously directing attention and energy henceforth. Where reactive thought patterns unconsciously sabotaged goals before, we now summon strategies.

The key is maintaining self-awareness when old narratives arise, noticing perfectionism or imposter syndrome rearing up. Label anxieties without judgment before purposefully pivoting attention back onto meaningful objectives within reach using the many techniques uncovered—progress eclipses paralysis.

By lovingly catching ourselves when stuckness recurs and then redirecting one baby step at a time, each of us holds the capacity to reinvent daily experience into aligned outcomes embodying potential. Tiny gains compound providing their own inspirational fuel in time. With compassion and patience, space opens for dreams to systematically transition from imagination into external reality through the progress portal.

I encourage you to review this book's motivational frameworks when discouragement strikes or perfectionism stalls efforts. Post reminder quotes by your workspace pulling insight from these pages, awakening your courage. But listen most for intuition's quiet voice urging you onward.

No matter the struggles faced, may you remember your intrigues and talents that called this book into your hands, eager for actualization. They may unfold through achievements seen as outstanding by the world or humble joys no less meaningful than nurturing those near to you. Define success on your own terms through aligned action.

By understanding the psyche's mysteries and our emotional obstacles now illuminated, we accept struggles as necessary for growth yet ephemeral in import relative to vision's victorious end. I have deep faith that your capable mindset shifts, motivation ignitions, habit resets, and accountability structures shall compound in their due time when fiercely tended as planted seeds.

Yes, progress requires surrendering the illusion of control while finding leverage to incrementally guide destiny's flow as favorably as possible. But simultaneously, what powerful agency rests in our hands the moment we choose affirmatively forward movement! However gradual, each micro-step elevates.

So now emerges an opportunity rife for seizing. May you go forward utilizing these pages' strategies to intentionally create days brimming with passion, meaning, and positive influence through consistent action. But pause amid the hustle to revisit the big picture frequently and adjust accordingly to what fundamentally satisfies.

With compassion for all facets of our shared human condition, yet convicted by dreams within urging actualization, let's now venture beyond old constraints into new horizons, unveiling wider vistas of what might become.

Bonus Chapter: Overcoming Imposter Syndrome

Many ambitious high-achievers secretly grapple with intense feelings of being intellectual frauds. Despite outward wins and praise, they believe success stems from lucky breaks rather than genuine ability. This phenomenon, termed "imposter syndrome," haunts even the most accomplished, making them feel like utter frauds soon to be exposed.

Imposter syndrome commonly breeds prolific anxiety and self-doubt. People feel they must work relentlessly to prevent perceived incompetence from being uncovered. Ironically, this links to procrastination risk, as avoiding finishing projects avoids possible failure exposure. Additionally, falsely feeling like undeserving frauds corrodes people's self-confidence to push past obstacles. Why keep trying if you secretly doubt having authentic talent despite accomplishments?

Insidiously, an outward persona rarely reveals inner turmoil. Onlookers see capable leaders, creatives, and speakers. But under the surface, many high-achievers minimize triumphs while inflating perceived individual deficits relative to peers. The mirror reflects capability while the mind screams inadequacy.

Often, these fraudulent feelings and perceived unworthiness derive from intersecting obstacles like perfectionism, harsh self-criticism, and comparison fixation. Through science-backed tactics illuminated here, including accumulating tangible wins, purposeful community, and self-compassion, we can start constructing unshakable self-confidence and self-efficacy from the inside out. Bold visions manifest through taking small but brave, tangible steps forward today.

Roots of Imposter Syndrome

Perfectionism often underpins imposter syndrome, as both center on feeling intrinsically flawed while placing unreasonable performance burdens on oneself. Perfectionists set extremely high standards for themselves. When they make even small mistakes or create average work instead of outstanding work, they view these as irreparable failures rather than opportunities to learn and grow. So, every less-than-genius result gets interpreted as proof of fraudulence rather than normal effortful progress.

Additionally, those wrestling with imposter syndrome frequently struggle to regulate self-esteem through external validation cues, too. They look outward for applause and promotions to convince themselves of competence versus building inner stability through growth mindsets. But the moment praise even slightly dips, fraudulent feelings return. Relying on external benchmarks proves shaky grounding.

Habitual social comparison tendencies only exacerbate the problem for those feeling like imposters. Viewing classmates and colleagues possessing skills not yet your own falsely confirms permanent deficiency rather than signaling areas for deliberate skill-building. Black-and-white thinking closes the possibility for gradual betterment.

Consequences of Imposter Fears

When left unchecked, the consequences of feeling like undeserving frauds long-term can sabotage careers through anxiety, self-doubt, and risk avoidance. As imposter fears grow, tasks begin feeling emotionally loaded minefields, exposing inadequacy. So, people self-sabotage through distraction or procrastination to avoid finishing projects up to imagined standards. Of course, this becomes a self-fulfilling prophecy cementing incompetence perspectives.

Additionally, imagined fraudulence often prevents going after advancement opportunities, precisely due to the dread of being revealed as less talented under increased spotlights. So potent professionals plateau early while less capable colleagues leapfrog them through bold ambition. By the time external applause confirms they do belong, imposter syndrome derails showcasing full talents. It's an endless anxiety cycle of leakage stealing oxygen for actualization.

Procrastination and delay provide temporary relief from the discomfort of feeling like an imposter but ultimately reinforce perceived fraudulence when important goals remain unfinished. Fear of failure leads to self-sabotage and avoided effort, preventing the small wins essential for constructing genuine confidence beyond surface accolades. It is an insidious cycle robbing personal potential.

Imposter Syndrome Manifesting as Procrastination

Imposter syndrome can manifest in profoundly debilitating procrastination and avoidance for even the most talented and capable. By creating intense inner turmoil regarding ability, fraudulent feelings, short-circuit motivation, plus follow-through on important goals.

Often, those secretly believing themselves to be unqualified frauds feel profound anxiety when ambitious projects arise requiring sustained effort and faith in talent. Whether plum leadership assignments, crafting genius grant proposals, or finally penning books simmering for years, self-doubt strikes envisioning personal visions actualized successfully by inadequate pretenders, namely themselves.

"I'm sure to bomb speaking on that global conference panel with such esteemed thought leaders and pioneers. I have nothing novel to add, so better not risk embarrassment being discovered as an utter fraud."

Such damning inner narratives understandably spark avoidance rather than attempted progress. Fueled by imagined inadequacy, people overtly distract or unconsciously drift from the aligned effort, sensing threat in dedicated activation. Days slip by in a fog of negative rumination and dopamine-releasing abdication of responsibility, over-channeling temporary relief from imagined fraud confrontation.

Weeks pass without tangible creation toward once-treasured aims as avoidance addiction intensifies. Each pang of yearning to view peers boldly risking vulnerability through publishing books, advancing companies, or unveiling creative gifts scratching procrastinated personal itches spurs despair, witnessing dreams mummify from comparative inaction.

We all struggle with motivation, follow-through, and confronting discomfort, even without fraudulent notions corroding self-efficacy. But undeniably, imagining ourselves as unqualified imposters destined for failure as pretenders invites full identity exposure and exponentially magnifies reasons for delay.

We can unlock wasted talent lost to perfectionism by first practicing extreme self-compassion. Even the most accomplished people struggle secretly with crippling self-doubt that fuels procrastination. Validating our own efforts leads to reclaiming our potential. We can then reconnect with our true passions that give life meaning. This internal compass matters more than meeting unrealistic perfectionistic standards. When guided by what intrinsically motivates us, we no longer strive for external validation. From that place of spirit alignment, small imperfect steps no longer intimidate. We walk the path for clues, discovering what gifts emerge through sustained, courageous action despite lingering insecurities.

Forward motion itself unblocks genius awaiting activation on the other side of long-avoided goals. With consistent devotion to micro-movement and closing emotional distance from imagined fraudulence notions, our greatness gets revealed as self-concepts evolve, reconciling accomplishments with mirages of unworthiness once paralyzing initiative.

Organizational Cultures Breeding Imposter Procrastination

Beyond personal psychology, toxic organizational dynamics can profoundly exacerbate imposter syndrome, leaking into procrastination, too. Environments punishing failure, scarce promotion pathways, or lack of psychological safety openly discussing insecurities create ripe conditions for imagined fraudulence to mushroom, delaying execution.

Often, fast-growth startups or competitive creative agencies reward superhuman endurance, wearing work martyrdom as a badge of honor. Showing vulnerability is often seen as a weakness. So people hide their flaws and overwork themselves to seem perfect, yet have no breathing room. Admitting uncertainty risks role stability when culture values outcomes above people.

This forces even top talent secretly wrangling fears of inadequacy to overcompensate through theatrical displays of hustle bravado, masking inner experiences of feeling continually outmatched or outlearned by teams decades younger. Rather than expose perceived fraudulence by asking questions or taking project sabbaticals to upskill, they pile busyness, filling skill gaps until they are overwhelmed. Only then comes buckling beneath unsustainable work volumes through anxiety leaves, passive role drift or sudden workplace dropouts once procrastinated pressures explode.

Everyone loses when cultural psychosis is warped by runaway capitalism forces covering authentic human struggles like imposter syndrome or exhaustion until it is too late. Rather than sustainably developing people for long careers harnessing hard-won wisdom, such organizations chew up passionate emerging leaders chasing innovation at human health expense.

The solution requires cultural revolutions centered on psychological safety to normalize struggle voicing, mutual mentorship beyond siloed teams, and career development paths honoring continually evolving mastery over missionary exhaustion glamorization.

When leaders open up about their own vulnerabilities, struggles, and growth, it organically changes culture for the better. Instead of pressure to seem invincible and perfect, people become more comfortable asking for help and embracing grit over perfection. Sharing stories that show it's okay to still be learning fosters adaptation and celebrates progress. Suddenly, imposter notions lose toxicity when universality is known. Coworkers bond supportively through common insecurity, which is no longer hidden, denying timely support.

With imposter syndrome destigmatized culturally and mentor squads actively demystifying unfamiliar skills urgently needed, talented teams access knowledge collaboratively to uplevel collectively. Failure gets reframed as iterative learning data versus threats jeopardizing jobs. Procrastination no longer strains to cover uncertainty when psychological safety blankets progress attempts imperfect but improving.

Workplace well-being utterly transforms when people walk partners on a journey toward purpose over product. Environments allow human cultures to realize their potential.

Perfectionism and Procrastination Risks

Perfectionism fueled by imposter syndrome profoundly amplifies procrastination susceptibility by paralyzing initiative through unrealistic internal quality standards. Here, people don't believe even their highest effort remotely approaches "good enough" to dare to share publicly or blaze trails toward actualizing potential.

Such perfectionists agonize endlessly over project details, sidelining executable progress for eventuality excellence. They reflexively discount work as inadequate despite external affirmation unless it meets unrealistic inner yardsticks.

For example, an entrepreneur writhing over website copy flaws prevents launching online courses teaching hard-won industry insights. Or paralyzing self-doubt scraps an entire manuscript after receiving interest from a literary agent.

Each time dreams demand public vulnerability declaring intellectual talents, familiar insecurity tape loops: "Who am I to profess expertise here?" Even extensive credentials can't silence whispers wondering: "What if people see through my facade of competence once products launch?"

Perfectionists put off taking career actions, even though waiting has high costs. They'd rather stay stuck behind the scenes than risk putting out half-finished work. In their minds, exposing any flaws would confirm deep fears of being unqualified to formally teach or lead others. Though irrational, this inner critique paralyzes them from sharing their gifts through products or offers.

It's an insidious cycle whereby every great imaginative concept immediately collapses under crippling scrutiny over landing pages misaligned by two pixels, income calculator formulas missing decimals, or course curriculum outlines not resembling Ivy League treatises.

Unquestionably, everything could be more refined. But when perfectionism breeds procrastination, eventually, we must challenge the necessity of pristine conditions to ever start sharing vulnerable gifts now versus perpetually postponed for impossible standards eventually or, you know, never.

Escaping requires identity shifts from self-worth tied to flawlessness toward courageous lifelong growth through consistent action full of micro-mistakes. We build motivation by starting small and then patiently polishing the work in progress. Each tiny gain accumulation fosters authentic confidence beyond applause, proving latent extraordinariness behind imperfect starts.

With supportive mentors and partners, we can find the courage to share unfinished work. We declare ourselves eternal students—refining as we go, not done but doing. Gentle patience allows our talents to unfold in their own time. Our early efforts may seem ramshackle, but they are real and full of potential. When acted upon steadily, our imperfect progress transforms lives, including our own.

Strategies to Overcome Imposter Syndrome

Thankfully, ample science-backed tactics exist for constructing unshakable self-confidence that dismantles fraudulent inner narratives over time. Strategies include:

Cataloging small wins frequently provides concrete proof of counteracting imagined fraudulence. Track accomplishments like positive customer feedback, goals hit ahead of schedule, and talents praised by colleagues. Stack enough micro-evidence, and imposter notions shrink.

Journal non-judgmentally about professional peak moments showcasing abilities and intellect. Capture what exactly made the thinking or performance demonstratively strong in detail. Re-read entries before intimidating projects or when doubting qualifications. Ground yourself in facts.

Seek out mentors and colleagues who model humble self-assuredness amidst challenges. Observe how confident competence walks and talks. Notice how they handle insecurity with compassion, not self-attack. Internalize wisdom through osmosis and conversation.

Additionally, reframe perceiving yourself as an imposter as a common transitional illusion on the growth arc toward full competency. External markers often proclaim our talents before internal metrics catch up. Give space for self-perception to unfold beyond harsh self-critique.

Perhaps most pivotal is the nurturing of the psychological concept of self-efficacy, the belief in one's fundamental capacity to accomplish goals and handle snags through resilient effort. Even small incremental progress confirms and compounds dormant potential into full manifestation. Tiny wins predict enormous growth.

Cultivating Unshakable Self-Confidence

Beyond concrete skill-building, transforming imposter syndrome at its root requires cultivating unshakable self-confidence internally to handle external evaluation turbulence. Potent methods:

Loosening dichotomous thinking patterns about intellectual adequacy is essential. Seeing competency as fixed black-and-white blocks growth pathways for incrementally improving abilities over time. But through growth mindset lenses, we interpret early project struggles as feedback for progress.

Equally important, meet occasional stumbles with self-compassion, not merciless criticism of normal missteps. Talk to yourself as a trusted mentor would, with empathy, remind yourself of your inherent talents. Self-care defuses destructive perfectionism, feeding fraudulent feelings.

To sustain self-assurance longer-term, proactively anchor identity narratives in actual strengths and values versus transient external applause. Catalog authentic wins frequently as proof of emerging excellence. Bold vision boarding solidifies self-concept for withstanding inevitable human vulnerabilities.

Takeaways and Next Steps

In closing, by applying the evidence-based strategies illuminated here, those secretly feeling like imposters can gradually dismantle fraudulent notions threatening to sabotage their highest potential day to day. Catalog micro-wins, speak with self-compassion, and crystallize identity through incremental progress. Your inner truths blaze brightly with consistent courage despite residual insecurities. Right now marks a pivotal opportunity to walk confidently into your next bold chapter, no longer hijacked by false notions of unworthiness!

Assessment: Your Imposter Procrastination Profile and Customized Turnarounds

Discover your unique imposter procrastination profile by choosing the most relatable response to the situations below. Then, review common emotional root causes and personalized turnaround strategies to start regaining momentum if these resonate.1.

Tough work projects arise, causing me to:

A) Endlessly refine details, fearing imperfect work would confirm I'm an inadequate fraud if launched publicly.

B) Distract myself by watching TV to numb the nagging inner voice, saying I'll fail inevitably, so why bother trying?

C) Overwork obsessively to overcompensate for anxieties around lacking skills to meet sophisticated expectations.

Root Causes: Perfectionism, perceived fraudulence, self-efficacy doubts.

Customized Turnarounds:

If A, commit to shipping incomplete work by certain dates for constructive feedback accepting imperfection—progress over perfection.

If B, divide big goals into miniature milestones, building tangible competence fuel, countering negative narratives.

If C, request a mentor relationship with a leader adept at setting nurturing expectations that stretch abilities without overburdening.

Getting positive feedback, I tend to:

A) Minimize praise, discounting achievements as flukes I can't replicate reliably, proving my incompetence eventually.

B) Feel uplifted briefly before familiar fraud notions resurface, saying, "They'd retract acclaim if knowing I'm winging it!"

C) Receive validation externally but can't internalize it emotionally since accomplishments never feel outstanding enough to deserve lauds.

Root Causes: Fraudulence notions, validation seeking, distorted self-perception.

Customized Turnarounds:

If A, reframe ability as learnable through dedication, not a fixed trait. We grow in competence through practice over time.

If B, record verbal praise from others to replay combating inner critic. Evidence builds credible new identity stories.

If C, connect and share openly with mentors who've overcome feeling inadequately accomplished despite external proof. Community normalizes growth curves.

Concerning big future goals I'd love to achieve, I tend to:

A) Sabotage through distraction numbing self-doubt, I could ever attain a vision that meaningfully impacts lives.

B) Hesitate initially starting intimidating tasks, paralyzed by anxiety around failing publicly if I aimed that ambitiously.

C) Strategize endlessly around the person I'd need to become to possibly deserve an actualizing concept that feeds the soul

Root Causes: Fraud fears, perfectionism, perceived unworthiness.

Customized Turnarounds:

If A, break the project into tiny incremental tasks, building tolerated momentum toward my vision despite uncertainty.

If B, frame paralysis as a common learning curve, not a personal shortcoming. Follow mini-step courage daily.

If C, release attachment to qualifiers needing meeting. Take small actions, letting the path reveal the true north vocational indicators over time.

Now, harnessing deeper awareness around your unique procrastination obstacles and customized turning points, what resonates as one manageable next step in applying relevant learnings into reality? Build on that empowered shift to incrementally transform relationships with inadequacy narratives formerly preventing drive toward expansive self-actualization!

Takeaways and Next Steps

Let's review foundational insights uncovered for constructing unshakable self-confidence beyond imposter syndrome:

- Fraudulent feelings often derive from perfectionism, validation dependence, and social comparison habits that warp self-perception.

- Consequences can include anxiety, self-sabotage through procrastination, and lost advancement opportunities.

- Science-backed antidotes exist, such as tracking micro-wins as proof of competence and seeking mentors modeling secure self-assuredness.

- Beyond skills, cultivating self-compassion and a growth mindset nourishes resilience to outer turbulence and questioning credentials.

With a deeper understanding of common roots causing even the most talented at doubting legitimate abilities, we can catch and reframe distorted thoughts before they unleash procrastination paralysis and anxiety loops undermining our potential.

Take stock of personal obstacles most triggering fraudulent inner narratives for you currently, whether harsh self-criticism, comparison tendencies, or unrealistic standards. Then, commit to three small but consistent actions, building authentic confidence each day.

Maybe that means cataloging a weekly accomplishment, speaking an affirmation of self-acceptance out loud, or reflecting on positive feedback from others. Tiny steps accumulate into unstoppable self-trust. You've got this!

Case Study: Conquering Imposter Syndrome

Meet Robin, a talented eco-architect who won early acclaim for sculptural community spaces crafted from sustainable materials. Her award-winning designs blended functionality, aesthetics, and environmental justice beautifully.

Yet internally, Robin constantly battled fearful voices, minimizing her creative talents as mediocre despite external praise. During initial concept phases, imposter notions often sabotaged ideation flow by undermining self-confidence to explore novelty. She fixated on technical wizardry other architects demonstrated rather than intrinsic design abilities.

Afraid brilliant ideas would expose inadequacy if attempted; Robin resorted to procrastination and distraction rather than pushing past paralyzing anxiety onto drafting boards. Finally, a respected mentor named Gabe, newly retired yet eager to nurture next-generation talents, detected Robin's fraudulent anxieties and bleeding passion from her process.

Through deep listening sessions, Gabe helped Robin intercept distorted narratives as they arose during collaborations. He assisted in reframing struggles as inherent to the nonlinear drafting process rather than personal flaws if initial renderings seemed uninspired. Support plus a reframed mindset helped Robin battle uncertainty-triggered procrastination.

Soon, Robin initiated documenting small daily creation wins in a progress journal, noting technical skills honed through practice. Concrete accomplishment visibility oppressed fraudulent notions over time as completed projects accumulated. Three months later, Robin landed dream clients advancing equitable housing after proposal confidence conquered former imposter blocks.

She still battles occasional self-doubt, hearing colleagues discuss high-tech capabilities. But a growth mindset plus palpable portfolio progress currently overpower fraudulent feelings. Robin's self-efficacy is cemented through the consistent manifestation of vision despite lingering insecurities.

Exercise: Confronting Your Inner Fraud Police

Let's shine some investigative light on personal obstacles enabling those fraudulent inner voices currently:

Make a list of three to five recent professional or creative moments you felt like an imposter, underserving of praise, or incapable of repeating high-level performance.

For each scenario, dig deeper, asking, "What core doubts or insecurities get triggered here?" Do you feel intrinsically flawed? Fear criticism if you fail to meet perfectionist standards? Worry you don't authentically belong with accomplished peers?

Now, list three small weekly actions building genuine self-efficacy to drown out fraudulent notions. Maybe that means cataloging a micro-win, voice recording an affirmation of self-acceptance, or reflecting on positive feedback from a mentor.

Choose consistent confidence-building actions that feel most authentic and doable. Stack enough evidence through commitment and courage facing fears, and soon self-trust rises to meet those former imposter notions with calm assuredness. The path awaits your brave steps forward!

Journaling Exercise:

Make a two-column table with "I feel like a fraud when_____" on the left and "I reassure myself by_____" on the right. Practice rewriting fearful inner narratives.

Affirmation:

"Through small steps forward now, I confidently claim my capability and worthiness."

Action Step:

Identify a formerly intimidating goal recently delayed by imposter notions. Commit to one imperfect baby step toward it, however tiny!

Wrapping Up...

As we conclude our journey illuminating imposter syndrome's common roots and transformational solutions, let's recall key milestones covered:

We explored how fraudulent feelings often derive from impossible standards, validation addiction, and comparison habits that distort self-perception over time. Critical inner voices undermine accomplishments.

Consequences can include anxiety, procrastination, and self-sabotage to avoid revealing perceived incompetence as well as lost advancement opportunities. It is an endless cycle of deteriorating mental health and potential without intervention.

Thankfully, science validates concrete tactics like tracking micro-wins as proof of competence and seeking out mentors who model grounded self-assurance. We also cultivate self-compassion to handle imperfections and anchor identity to actual strengths versus performance.

Each small step forward constructively builds self-efficacy, the growing belief in one's intrinsic capacity to handle goals and setbacks. Progress embeds neural pathways, confirming confidence subtly over time.

While insecurities may always arise on ambitious journeys, applying strategies here allows for the gradual dismantling of notions of fraudulence threatening our highest potential. We walk forward boldly while acknowledging residual doubts with compassion rather than judgment. And through consistent courage despite residual fears, previously intimidating visions unfold victorious.

You've got this! Right now marks a pivotal opportunity to walk confidently into your next chapter, no longer hijacked by secret feelings of unworthiness. Your inner truths blaze brightly each time you summon bravery in their name.

Thank You for Your Support!

Dear Reader,

We extend our heartfelt gratitude for choosing "How to Overcome Procrastination" as part of your reading journey. Your support means the world to us.

🌟 Your Opinion Matters!

If you've enjoyed the book and found it valuable, we would greatly appreciate it if you could take a moment to share your thoughts with us. Your feedback is crucial in helping us improve and in guiding future readers.

📑 Leave a Review

Your honest review will not only inspire us but also assist others in making an informed decision. Thank you for being a part of this literary adventure.

Warm regards,
Aria Ponder

References

Beutel, M. E., Klein, E. M., Aufenanger, S., Brähler, E., Dreier, M., Müller, K. W., Quiring, O., Reinecke, L., Schmutzer, G., Stark, B., & Wölfling, K. (2016). Procrastination, distress and life satisfaction across the age range – A German Representative Community Study. *PLOS ONE, 11*(2). https://doi.org/10.1371/journal.pone.0148054

Budson, A. (2021, May 13). *Can mindfulness change your brain?* Harvard Health. https://www.health.harvard.edu/blog/can-mindfulness-change-your-brain-202105132455

Cherry, K. (2021, July 4). *The zeigarnik effect is why you keep thinking of unfinished work.* Verywell Mind. https://www.verywellmind.com/zeigarnik-effect-memory-overview-4175150

Rogers, S. (2023, September 8). *Overcoming setbacks - teach better.* Teach Better. https://teachbetter.com/blog/overcoming-setbacks/

Shatz, I. (2019). *Why people procrastinate: The psychology and causes of procrastination – Solving procrastination.* Solving Procrastination. https://solvingprocrastination.com/why-people-procrastinate/

Swider, B., Harari, D., Breidenthal, A. P., & Steed, L. B. (2018, December 27). *The pros and cons of perfectionism, according to research.* Harvard Business Review. https://hbr.org/2018/12/the-pros-and-cons-of-perfectionism-according-to-research

Tóth, R., Turner, M. J., Mannion, J., & Tóth, L. (2023). The effectiveness of rational emotive behavior therapy (REBT) and mindfulness-based intervention (MBI) on psychological, physiological and executive functions as a proxy for sports performance. *BMC Psychology, 11*, 442. https://doi.org/10.1186/s40359-023-01486-8

Vedantam, S. (2023, December 8). *A quick trick for better focus*. Hidden Brain. https://news.hiddenbrain.org/p/a-quick-trick-for-better-focus

Visser, L., Korthagen, F. A. J., & Schoonenboom, J. (2018). Differences in learning characteristics between students with high, average, and low levels of academic procrastination: students' views on factors influencing their learning. *Frontiers in Psychology, 9*. https://doi.org/10.3389/fpsyg.2018.00808

Yan, B., & Zhang, X. (2022). What research has been conducted on procrastination? Evidence from a systematical bibliometric analysis. *Frontiers in Psychology, 13*.
https://doi.org/10.3389/fpsyg.2022.809044APA